S0-EEJ-587

Engaging Iran and Building Peace in the Persian Gulf Region

A Report to
The Trilateral Commission

European Author
VOLKER PERTHES

North American Author
RAY TAKEYH

Pacific Asian Author
HITOSHI TANAKA

Published by
The Trilateral Commission
Washington, Paris, Tokyo
2008

The Trilateral Commission was formed in 1973 by private citizens of Europe, Japan, and North America to foster closer cooperation among these three democratic industrialized regions on common problems. It seeks to improve public understanding of such problems, to support proposals for handling them jointly, and to nurture habits and practices of working together. The Trilateral countries are nations in Europe, North America, and Pacific Asia that are both democratic and have market economies. They include the member and candidate member nations of the European Union, the three nations of North America, Japan, South Korea, the Philippines, Malaysia, Indonesia, Singapore, Thailand, Australia, and New Zealand.

These essays were prepared for the Trilateral Commission and are distributed under its auspices. The European author held consultations in Tehran during February 2–7, 2008. The essays were discussed at the Commission's annual meeting in Washington on April 27, 2008.

The authors—from North America, Europe, and Pacific Asia—have been free to present their own views. The opinions expressed are put forward in a personal capacity and do not purport to represent those of the Trilateral Commission or of any organization with which the authors are or were associated.

Library of Congress Cataloging-in-Publication Data

Perthes, Volker.
  Engaging Iran and building peace in the Persian Gulf Region : a report to the Trilateral Commission / European author Volker Perthes, North American author Ray Takeyh, Pacific Asian author Hitoshi Tanaka.
    p. cm. -- (The triangle papers ; 62)
  ISBN 978-0-930503-91-8
  1. Iran--Politics and government--1997- 2. Iran--Strategic aspects. 3. Iran--Foreign relations--1997- 4. Persian Gulf Region--Politics and government--21st century. I. Takeyh, Ray, 1966- II. Tanaka, Hitoshi, 1947- III. Title.
  DS318.825.P47 2008
  955.06--dc22

                              2008038357

The Trilateral Commission

www.trilateral.org

1156 15th Street, NW   5, Rue de Téhéran
Washington, DC 20005   75008 Paris, France

Japan Center for International Exchange
4-9-17 Minami-Azabu
Minato-ku
Tokyo 106, Japan

Contents

The Authors

European Author

Volker Perthes has been chairman and director of the German Institute for International and Security Affairs (SWP) in Berlin since 2005. He was senior research associate at SWP and head of Middle East and Africa Research Group from 1992 until March 2005. In 1991–1993, he was assistant professor at the American University of Beirut. His areas of expertise include German and European foreign and security policy, transatlantic relations, and the Middle East. Dr. Perthes has written numerous books, his most recent being *Oriental Promenades: The New and Middle East in Flux* (2007).

North American Author

Ray Takeyh is a senior fellow for Middle Eastern studies at the Council on Foreign Relations. His areas of specialization are Iran, the Persian Gulf, and U.S. foreign policy. He is also a contributing editor of the *National Interest.* Dr. Takeyh was previously professor of national security studies at the National War College; professor and director of studies at the Near East and South Asia Center, National Defense University; fellow in international security studies at Yale University; fellow at the Washington Institute for Near East Policy; and fellow at the Center for Middle Eastern Studies, University of California, Berkeley. Dr. Takeyh is currently working on a book entitled *The Guardians of the Revolution: Iran's Approach to the World* (under contract by Oxford University Press). He is the author of a number of books including *Hidden Iran: Paradox and Power in the Islamic Republic* (Times Books, 2006) and *The Origins of the Eisenhower Doctrine: The U.S., Britain and Nasser's Egypt, 1953–1957* (MacMillan Press, 2000). Dr. Takeyh earned a doctorate in modern history from Oxford University.

Pacific Asian Author

Hitoshi Tanaka is a senior fellow at the Japan Center for International Exchange and was deputy minister for foreign affairs of Japan until August 2005. He had earlier been director general of the Asian and Oceanian Affairs Bureau (2001–2002) and the Economic Affairs Bureau (2000–2001); consul general in San Francisco (1998–2000); and deputy director general of the North American Affairs Bureau (1996–1998). He was director for policy coordination of the Foreign Policy Bureau; political minister at the Japanese embassy in London (1990–1993); a research associate at the International Institute for Strategic Studies, London (1989–1990); director for North East Asian affairs (1987–1989); and director for North American affairs (1985–1987). He has a B.A. in law from Kyoto University and a B.A.–M.A. in philosophy, politics, and economics from Oxford University.

1

Iran's Place in the Greater Middle East: Historical Overview

Ray Takeyh

A state's international orientation is shaped by a variety of factors and historic interactions. Cultural traits, ideological aspirations, demographic pressures, and religious convictions are all critical in determining how a country views its environment and its place within its neighborhood. Iran is no exception, as its unique national narrative and Islamic pedigree define its approach to the Greater Middle East.

As with most revolutionary states, Iran has journeyed from being a militant actor challenging regional norms to being a more pragmatic state pursuing a policy based on national-interest calculations. However, Iran's journey has been halting, incomplete, and tentative. Through the 1980s, under the stern dictates of Ayatollah Ruhollah Khomeini, Iran thrashed about the Middle East, seeking to undermine established authority in the name of Islamic redemption. Khomeini's successors would wrestle with this legacy, as they sought to integrate the theocracy into global society. From Ali Akbar Hashemi Rafsanjani to Muhammad Khatami to Mahmoud Ahmadinejad, Iran's presidents would seek the impossible, balancing Khomeini's vision with the mandates of the international community.

The best manner of understanding Iran's regional policy is to envision three circles: the Persian Gulf, the Arab East, and Eurasia. By far, the Persian Gulf would be the most significant, while the Arab East and Central Asian lands would assume lessened importance. The intriguing aspect of Tehran's policy is that although ideology may define its approach toward one of these circles, in the others, careful national-interest determinations would prove its guide. Thus, while in the 1980s the Saudis decried Iran as a grave fundamentalist threat, Russian diplomats just as convincingly testified to Tehran's pragmatism and moderation. Such a bewildering array of policies and priorities has often confounded the international community, making Iran's foreign policy difficult to comprehend. Through a more detailed assessment of the evolution of Iran's regional policy, one can better appreciate why the clerical state has made the decisions that it has and where it is likely to go from here.

Sources of Iranian Conduct

More than any other nation, Iran has always perceived itself as the natural hegemon of its neighborhood. Iranians across generations are infused with a unique sense of their history, the splendor of their civilization, and the power of their celebrated empires. The Achaemenid Empire of the sixth century B.C. was, after all, the first global power, reigning imperiously over lands that stretched from Greece to India. Subsequent Persian dynasties of Sassanians and Safavids displayed similar imperial reach, as they intricately managed vast domains. A sense of superiority over one's neighbors—the benighted Arabs and the unsophisticated Turks—defined the core of the Persian cosmology. To be sure, that empire has shrunk over the centuries, and the embrace of Persian culture has faded with the arrival of the more alluring Western mores, but a sense of self-perception and an exaggerated view of Iran have remained largely intact. By dint of its history and the power of its civilization, Iranians believe that their nation should establish its regional preeminence.

Yet Iran's nationalistic hubris is married to a sense of insecurity derived from persistent invasion by hostile forces. The humiliating conquests by the Mongol hordes and Arabs have left Iran profoundly suspicious of its neighbors' intentions and motives. Few nations have managed to sustain their cultural distinction and even absorb their conquerors as effectively as the Persians. In due course, Persian scholars, scribes, and bureaucrats came to dominate the courts of Arab empires and define their cultural landscape. Nonetheless, such unrelenting incursions with their prolonged periods of occupation have had a traumatic impact, leading Iranians to simultaneously feel superior to and suspicious of their neighbors.

By far, the one set of imperial conquerors that proved the most formidable challenge to Iran were the Western powers. These states could neither be absorbed as the Arabs were, nor did they necessarily defer to Persians for the management of their realm. In a sense, Iran became another victim of the "Great Game," played by the British and the Russians for the domination of Central Asia, and later the intense Cold War rivalry between America and the Soviet Union. While it is true that Iran was never formally colonized as was India, nor did it undergo a traumatic national liberation struggle as did Algeria, it was still dominated and its sovereignty was still usurped by imperial intrigue. Behind every shah lay a foreign hand that could empower or humble the Peacock Throne with ease. The shahs and the parliaments debated and deliberated, but all Iranian politicians had to be mindful of the preferences of the imperial game masters. At times, a degree of autonomy would be secured by manipulating great-power rivalries, but this was a precarious exercise, as accommodation usually proved a better path toward self-preservation. Perhaps the Islamic Republic's stridency and suspicions of the international community can better be understood in the context of Iran's historic subjection and manipulation by outside powers.

To ascribe Iran's foreign policy strictly to its sense of nationalism and historical grievances is, however, to ignore the doctrinal foundations of the theocratic regime. Khomeini bequeathed to his successors an ideology in which the most salient division was between the oppressors and the oppressed. Such a view stemmed from the Shiite political traditions as a minority sect struggling under Sunni Arab rulers who were often repressive and harsh. Thus, the notion of tyranny and suffering has a powerful symbolic aspect as well as practical importance. Iran was not merely a nation seeking independence and autonomy within the existing international system. The Islamic revolution was a struggle between good and evil, a battle waged for moral redemption and genuine emancipation from the cultural and political tentacles of the profane and iniquitous West. Khomeini's ideology and Iran's nationalist aspirations proved reinforcing, creating a revolutionary, populist approach to the regional realities.[1]

The Islamic Republic's inflammatory rhetoric and regional aspirations conceal the reality of Iran's strategic loneliness. Iran is, after all, a Persian state surrounded by non-Persian powers, depriving it of the ethnic and communal ties so prevalent in the Arab world. If durable alliances are predicated on a common vision and shared values, then

---

1 Hamid Algar, *Islam and Revolution: Writings and Declarations of Imam Khomeini* (Berkeley: Mizan Press, 1981); Ali Akbar Velayati, *Iran va Mas'eleh-ye Felestin* (Tehran: Daftar-i Nashr-i Farhang-i Islami, 1997), 3–10.

Iran is destined to remain somewhat insulated from the rest of its region. Nor, until the emergence of the Shiite bloc in Iraq, has religion necessarily mitigated Iran's isolation. Historically, the persecuted Shiites have been held at arm's length by the Sunni Arabs, who harbor their own suspicions of their co-religionists. In a standard Persian self-justification, Iran has tried to turn its isolation into an advantage, as notions of self-sufficiency and self-reliance have had an emotive appeal to a beleaguered populace. Nonetheless, as Iran's rulers look over the horizon, they seldom see a placid landscape or ready-made allies.

Iran is a country of contradictions and paradoxes. It is both grandiose in its self-perception yet intensely insecure. It seeks to lead the region while remaining largely suspicious and disdainful of its neighbors. Its rhetoric is infused with revolutionary dogma, yet its actual conduct is practical, if not realistic. A perennial struggle between aspirations and capabilities, hegemony, and pragmatism has characterized Iran's uneasy approach to the Greater Middle East.

First Circle: The Persian Gulf

Despite the mullahs' often-declared pan-Islamic pretensions, the Persian Gulf has always been Iran's foremost strategic priority. The critical waterway constitutes Iran's most direct link to the international petroleum market, the lifeblood of its economy. Although the eight-year war with Iraq dominated Iran's concerns during the early revolutionary period, it is important to note that Tehran's concerns and aspirations in the Gulf transcend Iraq. The Islamic Republic, as with all its monarchical predecessors, perceived that Iran by virtue of its size and historical achievements has the right to emerge as the local hegemon. The changing dimensions of Iran's foreign policy are most evident in this area, as revolutionary radicalism has gradually yielded to pragmatic power politics.

Soon after achieving power, Khomeini called on the Gulf states to emulate Iran's revolutionary model and sever relations with the "Great Satan," the United States. The profligate princely class, the hard-pressed Shiite populations, and these states' dependence on the United States were all affronts to Iran's revolutionaries. The theocratic state unambiguously declared the monarchial order a source of oppression and tyranny. "Monarchy is one of the most shameful and disgraceful reactionary manifestations," Khomeini declared.[2] An authentic Islamic society could not prevail under the banner of monarchy, as the proper ruling elite were the righteous men of God. Thus, beyond their foreign policy alignments, the character of the Gulf regimes proved a source of objection to Iran's new rulers.[3]

As Iran settled on its course of enmity and radicalism, the kingdom of Saudi Arabia emerged as the subject of particularly venomous attacks. In a sense, the two states had much in common, as they both predicated their legitimacy on a transnational mission of exporting religion and safeguarding Islam. The natural competition between their contending interpretations of Islam was sufficient to ensure a tense relationship. To this pressure was added Saudi Arabia's close ties to the United States, further fueling Khomeini's already intense antagonism toward the House of Saud. "In this age, which is the age of oppression of the Muslim world at the hands of the U.S. and Russia and their puppets such as Al-Sauds, those traitors to the great divine sanctuary must be forcefully cursed," he said.[4] The Iranian revolutionaries saw the Saudis as not just sustaining the imperial encroachment of the United States in the Middle East but also employing a reactionary interpretation of Islam to sanction their hold on power.[5]

---

2 Cited in Ruhollah Ramazani, *Revolutionary Iran: Challenge and Response in the Middle East* (Baltimore: John Hopkins University Press, 1986), 29.

3 Christine Marschall, *Iran's Persian Gulf Policy* (London: Curzon, 2003), 62–100; Nader Entessar, "Superpowers and Persian Gulf Security: The Iranian Perspective," *Third World Quarterly* (October 1988); Roy Mottahedeh, "Shiite Political Thought and Destiny of the Iranian Revolution," in *Iran and the Gulf: A Search for Stability,* ed. Jamal Al-Suwaidi (Abu Dhabi: Emirates Center for Strategic Studies and Research, 1996), 70–81.

4 David Menashri, "Khomeini's Vision: Nationalism or World Order?" and Farhad Kazemi and Jo-Anne Hart, "The Shi'ite Praxis: Democratic Politics and Foreign Policy in Iran," in *The Iranian Revolution and the Muslim World,* ed. David Menashri (Boulder, Colo.: Westview, 1990); Graham Fuller, *The Center of the Universe: Geopolitics of Iran* (Boulder: Westview Press, 1991), 8–34; Marvin Zonis and Daniel Brumberg, *Khomeini: The Islamic Republic of Iran and the Arab World* (Cambridge: Harvard University, Center for Middle Eastern Studies, 1987), 31–37.

5 Marschell, *Iran's Persian Gulf Policy,* 146–179; John Calabrese, *Revolutionary Horizons: Regional Foreign Policy in Post-Khomeini Iran* (New York, St. Martin's Press, 1994), 45–73.

Tehran's mischievous efforts were not without success; in the early 1980s, demonstrations rocked Kuwait, Saudi Arabia, and Bahrain. In the end, however, Iran's revolutionary message proved attractive only to a narrow segment of the minority Shiite population. Even the sporadic Shiite demonstrations were not designed to emulate Iran's revolution, but were rather an expression of the Shiites' economic and political disenfranchisement. The protesters used the specter of Iranian subversion to press their claims and extract needed concessions from the ruling elite. The prevailing regimes, for their part, seemed to appreciate this reality; and after putting down the demonstrations by force, they opted for economic rewards as a means of restoring quiescence. This strategy essentially ended Iran's attempt to exploit Shiite grievances to launch a new order. Tehran would subsequently rely on violence and terrorism, practices that were bound to alienate the local populace.

A campaign of bombings—targeting embassies, industrial plants, and even oil installations—was soon attributed to Iranian-sponsored opposition groups. The states that were particularly targeted by Iran's new tactics were those with substantial Shiite populations, namely Kuwait, Bahrain, and Saudi Arabia. In many cases, the instrument of Iranian terrorism was the al-Dawa party, which has since become part of the ruling coalition in post-Saddam Iraq. All this is not to point out the irony of the United States empowering an Iranian-terrorist client but to suggest that Iran's revolutionary élan faded rapidly, forcing it to rely on terrorist tactics that would succeed in neither overthrowing the incumbent regimes nor enhancing its standing in the international community.[6]

By the time of Khomeini's death in 1989, Iran's revolutionary foreign policy had not achieved any of its objectives. Tehran's attempt to export its revolution had not merely failed, but it had led the Gulf states to solidify against Iran. Leading regional actors such as Saudi Arabia severed diplomatic ties with the Islamic Republic, while the sheikdoms put aside their historic enmities and came together in the Gulf Cooperation Council, an organization largely devoted to containing Iranian influence. Along these lines, the Arab princes and monarchs further solidified their security ties to the United States and generously subsi-

---

6 Ali-Akbar Velayati, "The Persian Gulf: Problems of Security," *The Iranian Journal of International Affairs* (Spring 1991); Muhammad Javad Larijani, "Iran's Foreign Policy: Principles and Objectives," *Iranian Journal of International Affairs* (Winter 1996).

dized Saddam Hussein's military in his war with Iran. The revolution without borders seemed uneasily confined within Iran's borders.

The 1990s will stand as one of the most important periods of transition for the Islamic Republic. The end of the prolonged war with Iraq and Khomeini's death suddenly shifted focus away from external perils to Iran's domestic quandaries. The specter of invading Iraqi armies had ensured a remarkable degree of political conformity and allowed the regime to mobilize the masses behind its exhortations of national resistance. Khomeini's undisputed authority and his hold on the imagination of the public allowed the state to deflect attention from its domestic deficiencies and feel safe from popular recrimination. The basis of the regime's legitimacy and authority would now have to change, as the Islamic Republic had to offer a reason for its rule beyond the catastrophic invasion of its territory and the moral claims of its clerical founder.

Along these lines, Iran's new pragmatic rulers, led by Ali Akbar Hashemi Rafsanjani, began discussing a regional security arrangement whereby the stability of the Gulf would be ensured by the local regimes as opposed to external powers. After Saddam's eviction from Kuwait in 1991 and the deflation of his power, the mullahs in Iran perceived a unique opportunity to establish their hegemony in the region. Instead of instigating Shiite uprisings and exhorting the masses to emulate Iran's revolutionary model, Tehran now called for greater economic and security cooperation. However, the success of this ambition was predicated on the withdrawal of U.S. forces. This was to be hegemony on the cheap, with Iran's preeminence recognized, the U.S. presence lessened, and a permanent wedge drawn between Iraq and the Arab Gulf states. The only problem with this proposal was that it remained fundamentally unacceptable to the sheikdoms to which Saddam's invasion of Kuwait had conveyed the danger of relying on imperious local regimes for their security.[7]

In essence, Iran's new stratagem conflicted with the Gulf states' survival tactics. The sheikdoms, with their perennial concern about the designs of their more powerful and populous neighbors, viewed with apprehension Tehran's penchant toward collective security. Although relations between Iran and the Gulf states did improve in terms of establishment of formal diplomatic ties and volume of trade, the local

---

7 Ibid.

princes were not about to sever ties with the United States in order to appease Iran. In line with their long-standing historic practice, they sought the protection of external empires against neighboring states that have often coveted their wealth and resources. In the aftermath of the Gulf War, the level of defense cooperation between the United States and the Gulf regimes significantly increased, with the United States enforcing the containment of Iraq and the no-fly zones from the military bases in Saudi Arabia and Kuwait. In the 1980s Iran's revolutionary radicalism had polarized the Gulf, and in the 1990s Iran's insistence that these states share its opposition to the U.S. presence proved a source of division and tension.

Once more, the failure of Iranian ambitions triggered reliance on terrorism and intimidation. If the Gulf leaders refused to sever ties with the United States, then perhaps violence directed against U.S. troops would lead Washington to voluntarily withdraw from the region. For the clerical regime, as well as much of the Middle East, the U.S. departure from Lebanon after the 1983 bombing of the Marine barracks was an indication that the United States was unwilling to accept casualties and that a spectacular act of violence could trigger America's exit. The presence of U.S. troops in Saudi Arabia proved tantalizing to the mullahs, as Riyadh had remained largely aloof from Iran's blandishments. The 1996 bombing of the Khobar Towers, housing U.S. military personnel, has been attributed to Tehran by Washington.[8] Given Iran's policy of pressing for eviction of U.S. forces through acts of violence, this claim has a degree of credibility. As with the Islamic Republic's previous acts of terrorism, once more its strategy of selective violence failed to achieve its ambitions.

In the end, Rafsanjani and his pragmatic allies did not fundamentally harmonize Iran's ties with its neighbors. To be sure, the Islamic Republic did dispense with much of its revolutionary radicalism and began to project the image of a judicious state basing its policies on careful calculations of national interest. However, Tehran's tense relationship with the United States and its insistence that the Gulf states share its antagonism undermined its own gestures of goodwill. When Iran fell back on its predictable response of terrorism, it essentially

---

8 This point has been particularly emphasized by Louis Freeh in *My FBI: Bringing Down the Mafia, Investigating Bill Clinton, and Fighting the War on Terror* (New York: St. Martin's Press, 2005).

ended the possibility of emerging as a critical player in its immediate neighborhood.

The most momentous change in Iran's regional policy came with the election of the reformist president, Muhammad Khatami, in 1997. Khatami's international perspective grew out of the debates and deliberations prevalent in Iran's intellectual circles. Many dissident thinkers and clerics were uneasy about the static nature of Iran's foreign policy and its evident inability to respond to the changing global and regional realities. The reformist perspective was not limited to making the theocracy more accountable to its citizenry; it also sought to end the Islamic Republic's pariah status and integrate Iran into global society. As with his political reforms, Khatami was drawing on the works of intellectuals outside a power structure that had grown stagnant and complacent.

In terms of his approach to the Gulf, Khatami appreciated that previous attempts at reconciliation with the sheikdoms had failed owing to Iran's dogmatic insistence that they share its hostility to the United States. In essence, Khatami compartmentalized Iran's relations. To be sure, Tehran continued to object to the U.S. military presence in the Gulf and persisted in calling for an indigenous network to displace the U.S. armada. However, the refusal of the Gulf states to embrace Iran's proposals did not trigger a counterreaction and unleashing of terror. Khatami was willing to normalize relations with the Gulf states despite their attachment to the United States. For all practical purposes, Iran was prepared to live in a Gulf whose balance of power was determined by the United States.

In a remarkable gesture, Supreme Leader Ayatollah Khamenei, successor to Khomeini, endorsed Khatami's initiative. In a speech to the gathering of Arab dignitaries at the Organization of Islamic Conference's 1997 meeting in Tehran, Khamenei plainly declared, "Iran poses no threat to any Islamic country."[9] Tehran's "vision statement," which was approved by Khamenei, recognized the sovereignty of local states and the inviolability of borders, and it pledged noninterference in the internal affairs of the incumbent regimes. The mystery lingers of why Khamenei so fundamentally departed from his established antagonism toward the Gulf princely elite. Certainly, the popular appeal of Khatami in his honeymoon period must have impressed the Supreme Leader to

---

9 *Christian Science Monitor,* February 25, 2000.

adjust his positions. Despite the fact that Khamenei's powers are not contested by elections or plebiscites, he has always been somewhat sensitive to public opinion and shifts in the popular mood. Moreover, despite his stern ideological predilections, Khamenei has historically exhibited sporadic bouts of pragmatism and must have sensed that Iran's lingering isolation in its immediate neighborhood was ill serving the country's interests. Gazing across the region, the Supreme Leader may have perceived that Khatami's elections offered Iran certain opportunities for mending fences and reconciliation with important states, such as Saudi Arabia. At any rate, Khamenei provided the essential backing that Khatami's diplomacy of reconsideration required.

Khatami's "good neighbor" diplomacy finally managed to rehabilitate Iran's ties with the local regimes. An entire range of trade, diplomatic, and security agreements was signed between the Islamic Republic and the Gulf sheikdoms. In this way, Khatami managed finally to transcend Khomeini's legacy and to displace his ideological antagonisms with policies rooted in pragmatism and self-interest. This is the impressive legacy that Iran's unnecessarily maligned president has bequeathed to the callow reactionaries that have succeeded him.[10]

Today, as a hard-line government consolidates its power and proclaims a desire to return to the roots of the revolution, there are dire warnings on the horizon. Both Washington policymakers and their European counterparts seem to suggest that the regime will once more resort to violence and terror to subvert its neighbors and export its Islamic revolution. Such alarmism overlooks Iran's realities. As we have seen, under Khatami's auspices, Iran's Gulf policy underwent a fundamental shift, with national-interest objectives as its defining factor. Irrespective of the balance of power between conservatives and reformers, Iran's regional policy is driven by fixed principles that are shared by all of its political elites.

This perspective will survive Iran's latest leadership transition. Although Ahmadinejad and his allies are determined to reverse the social and cultural freedoms that Iranians have come to enjoy during the reformist tenure, with regard to Persian Gulf issues the new president has

---

10 R. K. Ramazani, "The Emerging Iranian-US Rapprochement," *Middle East Policy* (June 1998); Mohsen Milani, "Iran's Gulf Policy: From Idealism to Confrontation to Pragmatism and Moderation," in *Iran and the Gulf: The Search for Stability,* ed. Jamal a-Suwaidi (Abu Dhabi: Emirates Center for Strategic Studies and Research, 1996).

stayed within the parameters of Iran's prevailing international policy. In his August 2005 address to the parliament outlining his agenda, President Ahmadinejad echoed the existing consensus, noting the importance of constructive relations with "the Islamic world, the Persian Gulf region, the Caspian Sea region and Central Asia."[11] Moreover, the most important voice on foreign policy matters, the Supreme Leader, has reiterated the same themes.[12] Unlike during the 1980s, Ahmadinejad's Iran has not embarked on attempts to subvert the sheikdoms and has not revived Iran's links to the Gulf terrorist organizations unleashing violence as a means of fostering political change.

Today, the political alignments of the Gulf are in constant change. The U.S. invasion of Iraq has facilitated the rise of Iran's most intimate Shiite allies to power. As the George W. Bush administration contemplated its attack on Iraq in the aftermath of the September 11 tragedies, it is unlikely that it appreciated how its plans would enhance Iran's stature and security. The Islamic Republic now stands as one of the principal beneficiaries of the regime-change policy of the United States. In assessing the ironies and paradoxes of the Middle East, however, one need not descend into a zero-sum game whereby any measure that benefits Iran is necessarily viewed as endangering U.S. interests. The fact is that much of the tension and instability that has afflicted the critical Persian Gulf region in the past three decades has stemmed from animosity between Iran and Iraq. The contested borders, proxy wars, and finally a devastating eight-year conflict between the two powers not only destabilized the Middle East but also threatened the global economy with its reliance on the region's petroleum resources. The new Iraq that is emerging from the shadow of the U.S. invasion is likely to coexist peacefully with its Persian neighbor. And that development is good not just for Iran and Iraq but also for the United States.

Second Circle: The Arab East

One of the more enduring ideological aspects of the Islamic Republic's international relations has been its policy toward the Arab East. The defining pillar of Iran's approach to this region has been its intense opposition to the state of Israel and the diplomatic efforts to normalize

---

11 Islamic Republic News Agency (IRNA), August 23, 2005.

12 *Sharq*, July 26, 2005.

relations between the Jewish state and its neighbors. Iran's strident ideological policy has been buttressed by strategic incentives, as its support for militant groups such as Hezbollah gives it a power to influence the direction of politics in the Levant and inject its voice in deliberations that would otherwise be beyond its control. Along this path, Iran has made common cause with the radical Syrian regime that shares its antipathy to Israel while it has alienated the key Egyptian state that has often sought to resolve the divisive Arab-Israeli conflict. So long as Iran's policy toward the Arab East remains immured in its conflict with Israel, Tehran is unlikely to edge toward the type of pragmatism that it has demonstrated in the Gulf.

On the surface, the high-profile visits and the wide variety of compacts and accords may give the impression that Iran and Syria are intimate allies sharing the same vision and embracing similar priorities. However, the ties between the two states are at best an alliance of convenience based on shared fears and apprehensions. For the past two decades, Iran's persistent animosity toward Israel has coincided with Syria's quest to exert pressure on the Israelis as a means of recovering lands lost during the 1967 war. While Iran's policy is driven by Islamist determinations, Syria is propelled forward by cold, strategic calculations. Tehran may view Hezbollah as a vanguard Islamist force struggling against the "Zionist entity," but for Damascus the Lebanese militant party is just another means of coercing Israel. As such, potential conflict between Iran and Syria looms large. Syria may yet accept an agreement that exchanges recognition of Israel for the recovery of the Golan Heights, while Iran's more ideologically driven hostilities are not predicated on territorial concessions.[13]

Beyond the issue of Israel, Iraq also constitutes a potential source of division between Syria and Iran. During Saddam Hussein's reign, the two powers shared yet another antagonist. The Syrian Baath Party long condemned the so-called revisionism of its Iraqi counterpart and viewed itself as the legitimate representative of the Arab socialist cause. The very secular objections of the Syrian regime were shared by the Iranian mullahs, whose own war with Saddam made them equally hostile to the Iraqi dictator. Once more, however, there are indications

---

13 Shireen Hunter, "Iran and Syria: From Hostility to Limited Alliance," in *Iran and the Arab World,* ed. Hooshang Amirahmadi and Nader Entessar (New York: St. Martin's Press, 1993).

that Iran's lone Arab alliance may not survive the changing politics of the Middle East.

Unlike the Iranian theocracy, Syria does not wish to see a further empowerment of religious forces, particularly Shiite actors, in Iraq. As a secular state that has waged a merciless war against its own Islamists, Syria finds the ascendance of religious parties in Iraq particularly disconcerting. As with most of the Sunni dynasties and republics of the region, Syria had hoped that Saddam's demise would somehow bring to power yet another Baathist amenable to the predilections of the secular Arab bloc. The intriguing aspect of Iraq's current tribulations is the extent to which Iran and Syria are on the opposite sides, with Damascus fueling the largely Sunni insurgency, while Tehran lends its support to the ruling Shiite parties. One state is hoping to destabilize Iraq through continued violence, while the other views the conventional political process as the best means of securing its national objectives.

In yet another paradox of the Middle East, what is increasingly binding Damascus and Tehran together is the Bush administration. The inability or unwillingness of Washington to substantively engage in the Arab-Israeli peace process and craft an agreement acceptable to Syria has made Iran an indispensable partner for Damascus. The relentless pressure brought on both parties by the Bush White House has compelled Iran and Syria to rely on each other as they face yet another common enemy. Nonetheless, developments in the region during the next several years may yet disentangle ties between these two unlikely allies. In the end, as a state that neighbors Israel, Syria will one day have to accept a territorial compromise with the Jewish state and end its prolonged and self-defeating conflict. However, an Iran that is beyond the reach of Israeli armor can afford its militancy and persist with its ideologically determined policies. In the meantime, as a secular state, Syria may find Iran's new Shiite allies in Iraq as objectionable as do the Saudis and Jordanians, who are loudly decrying the emergence of the "Shiite crescent." As the Middle East increasingly polarizes along sectarian lines, Syria will have to choose between its contentious alliance with Iran and its alignment of interest with the larger Arab bloc.

Whatever the vagaries of the Iranian-Syrian alliance, Egypt remains the epicenter of Arab politics. Egypt's population now exceeds that of the rest of the Arab East, and its geographic size dwarfs peripheral states such as Lebanon and Jordan. Moreover, Egypt's encounter with modernization is the longest, its industrial and educational structures the most extensive, and its cultural and intellectual output the most prolific. Cairo's influence has ebbed and flowed over the years, but it is hard to imagine Arab cohesion without Egypt's active leadership. Iran's tense relations with Egypt have drastically limited its influence in the Arab East. No alliance with Syria or patronage of Hezbollah can compensate for Tehran's estrangement from the most pivotal state in the region.[14]

Although many in the United States are accustomed to perceiving Iran as unrelentingly hostile to the United States, during the early part of the revolution, Iran's animosities were distributed more widely. For Khomeini and his followers, no leader symbolized the pusillanimity of the Arab political class more than the Egyptian president, Anwar al-Sadat. The Camp David accords ending Egypt's hostility toward Israel were bitterly denounced by Iranian clerics as a gesture of un-Islamic behavior, even apostasy. For Khomeini, the accords proved that Sadat was the purveyor of "false Islam" and an agent of Zionism. Sadat's warm embrace of the exiled shah (who spent the last days of his life in Egypt) further enraged the reigning Iranian clerics. Tehran's crass celebration of Sadat's assassin by naming a prominent street after him and even issuing a stamp commemorating the occasion in turn infuriated an Egyptian ruling elite that was already anxious about the potential of Iran's revolutionary Islam. These early policies established a certain legacy for Iran's relations with Egypt that would prove difficult to surmount. In the intervening decades, other events would intrude, buttressing the legacy of mistrust and animosity.[15]

The Iran-Iraq War further added fuel to the Iranian-Egyptian antagonism. For Cairo, which was ostracized by the Arab bloc because of its reconciliation with Israel, the war offered a unique opportunity to reassert its Arabism and to mend ties with its erstwhile allies. Soon after the war began, Egypt started furnishing arms to Iraq despite the fact that the two powers had spent decades bitterly vying for the leadership of the Arab Middle East. Beyond exploiting an opportunity to return to the Arab fold, Cairo's policy was designed to contain Iran's

---

14 Shahrough Akhavi, "The Impact of Iranian Revolution on Egypt," in *The Iranian Revolution: Its Global Impact,* ed. John Esposito (Miami: University Press of Florida, 1990); Nader Entessar, "The Lion and the Sphinx: Iranian-Egyptian Relations in Perspective," in *Iran and the Arab World,* ed. Hooshang Amirahmadi and Nader Entessar.

15 R. K. Ramazani, *Revolutionary Iran: Challenges and Responses in the Middle East* (Baltimore: Johns Hopkins University Press, 1986), 162–172.

revolution within its borders. An Iran that was preoccupied with the daunting challenges of a prolonged war was bound to be a less mischievous state. For the Islamic Republic, such policies were tantamount to Egypt effectively joining the war, congealing the clerical class's animus toward Cairo.

The aftermath of the war did not necessarily lead to a thaw in relations. The 1990s witnessed yet another radical divergence of perspectives between Tehran and Cairo. For the United States and Egypt, the defeat of Saddam's armies constituted an ideal time to resolve the Arab-Israeli conflict, while Iran perceived that the time was ripe for the advancement of its Islamic model. Militant Islam seemed an ideology on the ascendance, with Islamic jihad challenging the Egyptian regime, Hezbollah assuming a greater prominence in Lebanese politics, and the Islamic Salvation Front triumphing in democratic elections in Algeria. The Palestinian resistance that had historically been led by secular leftist parties was increasingly being spearheaded by violent Islamist organizations such as Hamas. For the Iranian mullahs, it seemed that the region was finally embracing Khomeini's message. While the Egyptian state was seeking to stabilize its domestic situation and persuade the Arab states to follow its path of reconciliation with Israel, Iran was actively promoting the fortunes of the emboldened Islamists.

In a sense, Egyptian President Hosni Mubarak's blaming of Iran for the surge of fundamentalism in Egypt and the wider Middle East was self-serving and convenient. Egypt has long struggled with Islamic radicalism, and the roots of the Islamist rage lay deep in the Egyptian society. After all, the most significant fundamentalist party in the Middle East, the Muslim Brotherhood, was born in Egypt in the 1930s and since then has found a ready audience across the region.[16] The fascination with Wahhabi Islam ought not to obscure the fact that the intellectual and tactical architects of al Qaeda are mostly Egyptians, led by the notorious second-in-command, Ayman al-Zawahiri.[17] Nonetheless, even the modest support that Iran did offer Egypt's religious extremists was

---

16 Richard Mitchell, *The Society of the Muslim Brothers* (Oxford: Oxford University Press, 1993), 1–12.

17 Fawaz Gerges, *The Far Enemy: Why Jihad Went Global* (Cambridge: Cambridge University Press, 2005), 119–115; Gilles Kepel, *The War for Muslim Minds: Islam and the West* (Cambridge: Belknap Press of Harvard University Press, 2004), 70–81.

sufficient to antagonize an Egyptian state that in the early 1990s was battling a very serious Islamic insurrection.

During the Khatami era there were attempts to relax the tensions with Egypt. It appeared, however, that such normalization was not a top priority for either state. Khatami's internal struggles and his attempts to reach out to the United States were sufficiently contentious to preclude yet another provocative diplomatic foray. In the meantime, the Mubarak regime was struggling with its own domestic challenges and with a foundering peace process, and so it was also disinclined to move forward aggressively.

Today, the relations between the two states may not be as inflammatory as during the early periods of the revolution, but they do seem frozen in time, as neither side seems inclined to press ahead. The hard-line Ahmadinejad regime is unlikely to normalize ties, as many conservatives in Iran have yet to forgive Egypt for the Camp David accords. The reactionary newspaper *Jumhuri-ye Islami* captured the sentiment of many on the right in noting, "Any form of political relations with Husni Mubarak is tantamount to getting digested into the system prepared and designed by America and Zionism in the region."[18] Given such sentiment within his support base, it is unlikely that Ahmadinejad can move forward toward more proper relations, despite his demonstrated inclination to do so.

In the Persian Gulf, the Islamic Republic finally appreciated after years of revolutionary radicalism that it could not have suitable relations with the Gulf sheikdoms unless it came to terms with Saudi Arabia. Such lessons have yet to be absorbed by the Iranian elite when it comes to the Arab East. The reality is that Iran cannot be part of the larger Middle Eastern landscape until it regularizes its relations with Egypt. Tactical alliances with a beleaguered Syrian regime and patronage of terrorist organizations such as Hezbollah will not ease Iran's path to the heart of the Arab world. Tehran can be mischievous and use terrorism and violence as a means of attracting attention to its claims and obstructing peace initiatives between Israel and the Arab bloc. For Iran to assert its influence in the region, it has to have a more constructive agenda than prefabricated Islamist slogans and hostility to the Jewish state. Hovering over this is the gradual fracturing of the Middle East along confessional lines, with Shiite Iran being increasingly pitted against the alarmed Sunni powers. The Islamic Republic may emerge as a critical

---

18 *Jumhuri-ye Islami,* November 21, 2005.

player in its immediate neighborhood, but as a non-Arab, Shiite state it is unlikely to ever become a significant actor in the Arab East.

Third Circle: Eurasia

In contrast with its policy toward the Persian Gulf and the Arab East, Iran's approach toward its northern and eastern neighbors has been one of sustained realism. The proximity to a strong Russian state and the prospect of commercial contracts and important arms deals have always injected a measure of pragmatism in Iran's policy. In a curious manner, despite its declared mission of exporting the revolution, the Islamic Republic has seemed perennially indifferent to the plight of the struggling Muslims in Central Asia. A beleaguered Iranian state requiring arms and trade and an aggrieved former superpower seeking profits and relevance have forged an opportunistic relationship that eschews ideology for sake of tangible interests. Nor is such pragmatism unique vis-à-vis Russia: when the theocracy has looked to Afghanistan, its priority has always been stability, not Islamic salvation. In essence, the fears of being isolated in the international arena and having Afghan troubles seep over its borders have compelled Iran's theocratic oligarchs to transcend their ideological exhortations and focus on achieving their practical objectives in the vast Eurasian landmass.

On the eve of the Islamic Revolution, Iran's prevailing foreign policy slogan was "neither East nor West." Khomeini was as contemptuous of Soviet communism as he was of Western liberalism, and he often denounced the Soviet Union in harsh and unyielding terms. Iran vocally condemned the Soviet invasion of Afghanistan and materially assisted the mujahedin's resistance to the occupation. On the domestic front, the mullahs relentlessly persecuted the Communist Tudeh Party and other leftist forces attracted to the Soviet model. For its part, Moscow proved a generous supplier of arms to Saddam Hussein as he waged his war of aggression against Iran, and Moscow often supported Iraq against Iran in various international forums.

Yet even as tensions were simmering, both sides seemed to veer away from active confrontation, as trade between the two powers continued to increase, and the Soviet Union was never without an extensive diplomatic representation in Tehran. In a manner radically different from its approach to the United States, the theocratic regime seemed to appreciate that its geographic proximity to the Soviet Union and its estrangement from the West required a more realistic relationship with Moscow. The two sides would often differ, as they did on critical issues of Afghanistan and Iraq, yet somehow Khomeini managed to suppress his ideological animosities and pursue ties with the Soviet state that seemed beneficial to Iran's overall interests.[19]

The collapse of the Soviet Union in 1991 and the rise of the Russian Federation ushered in a new regional policy in Moscow. The Soviet state had been inordinately invested in the fortunes of radical Arab regimes and shared their concerns regarding developments in the Arab-Israeli arena. For the new masters of the Kremlin, the direction of the newly independent Central Asian republics and the nature of Islamic awakenings in that region were far more relevant than the plight of the Soviet Union's Arab clients. The stability of the Russian frontier was now partly contingent on Tehran resisting the impulse to inflame Islamic sentiments in Central Asia. Moreover, with its imperial reach dramatically contracted and the country in dire need of hard currency, Russia began to auction off its military hardware to the highest bidders. Iran proved a tempting market for Russian arms merchants, as it possessed both cash and a seemingly insatiable appetite for military equipment.[20]

The Islamic Republic had to make its own set of adjustments to the collapse of the Soviet Union and the emergence of Central Asia. During the Soviet era, Iran had propagated its Islamic message over the airwaves in a variety of local languages without evident anticipation that it would have any impact. Such limited propaganda effort satiated its ideological imperatives without unduly straining its relations with its powerful neighbor. But the collapse of the Soviet empire and the independence of the Central Asian republics presented Iran with the need for circumspection. The Islamic Republic had to balance its strategic ties with Russia with its declared mission of exporting its revolutionary

---

19 Shireen Hunter, *Iran and the World: Continuity in a Revolutionary Decade* (Bloomington: Indiana University Press, 1990), 79–98; Graham Fuller, *The Center of the Universe*, 168–188.

20 Robert Freedman, "Russian Policy Toward the Middle East: The Yeltsin Legacy and the Putin Challenge," *Middle East Journal* (Winter 2001); Hooman Peimani, *Regional Security and the Future of Central Asia: The Competition of Iran, Turkey and Russia* (Westport, Conn.: Praeger, 1998), 41–129.

template to new, fertile grounds. In a unique display of judiciousness, Iran largely tempered its ideology, essentially denoting the importance of trade and stability over propagation of its Islamic message.[21]

The full scope of Iran's pragmatism became evident during the Chechnya conflict. At a time when the Russian soldiers were indiscriminately massacring Muslim rebels and aggressively suppressing an Islamic insurgency, Iran's response was a mere statement declaring the issue to be an internal Russian affair. At times, when Russia's behavior was particularly egregious, Iran's statements would be harsher. However, Tehran never undertook practical measures such as dispatching aid to the rebels or organizing the Islamic bloc against Moscow's policy. Given that Iran had calculated that its national interests lay in not excessively antagonizing the Russian Federation, it largely ignored the plight of the Chechens despite the Islamic appeal of their cause.[22]

The Chechnya issue reveals that during the past decade a tacit yet important bargain has evolved between Russia and Iran. The Islamic Republic has emerged as Russia's most important partner in the Middle East and as a valuable market for its cash-starved defense industries. Although in recent years the nuclear cooperation between the two states has garnered much attention, the more significant fact is that Russia has also been willing to sell Iran a vast quantity of conventional arms, including sophisticated aircraft and submarines. Iran, on the other hand, has kept a low profile in Central Asia and has refrained from destabilizing a region critical to Russia's security. This important relationship has led Moscow to provide Iran indispensable diplomatic support, particularly at a time when Iran's nuclear portfolio is being addressed in a variety of international organizations. The United States, hopeful of garnering Russian support for its policy of sanctioning and ostracizing Iran, would be wise to consider the overall nature of relations between Moscow and Tehran. Given that reality, the notion that Russia would assist in applying significant economic pressure on Iran for its nuclear infractions is far-fetched and fanciful.

---

21 Hanna Yousif Freij, "State Interests vs. the Umma: Iranian Policy in Central Asia, *Middle East Journal* (Winter 1996); Shireen Hunter, "Iran's Pragmatic Regional Policy," *Journal of International Affairs* (Spring 2003).

22 A. William Samii, "Iran and Chechnya: Realpolitik at Work," *Middle East Policy* (March 2001); Svante Cornell, "Iran and the Caucasus," *Middle East Policy* (January, 1998).

A similar penchant toward national-interest calculations has defined Iran's policy toward Afghanistan, its neighbor to the east. Despite Iran's close linguistic and cultural ties to Afghanistan, the relations between the two countries have not always been simple. The fiercely independent Afghan tribes have historically resisted Persian encroachment and have jealously guarded their rights. Tehran's most natural allies are found in the province of Herat, whose proximity to Iran and large Shiite population have welcomed the establishment of close relations. However, for Tehran the issue in Afghanistan has not been ideological conformity but stability. Since assuming power, the theocracy has looked warily upon its neighbor with its war against the Red Army, the rise of Taliban fundamentalism, and finally the U.S. invasion. Afghanistan's tribal identity, ethnic diversity, and largely Sunni population have made it an uneasy place for implanting the Islamic Republic's revolutionary message. And, to its credit, Iran has not been active in seeking to export its governing template to its troubled neighbor.

During much of the 1980s, Iran's policy toward Afghanistan was opposition to the Communist regime and assisting forces battling the Soviet occupation. In yet another uneasy paradox, the decade of the 1980s saw a rough coincidence of objectives between Iran and the United States as both parties had an interest in holding back Soviet power in Southwest Asia. Although Khomeini attempted to justify this policy on Islamic grounds, the instability of the war and the extension of Soviet influence southward offered sufficient strategic justification for Iran's conduct. At a time when Iran was housing nearly two million Afghan refugees, the clerical state understood that it could not afford a failed state next door.[23]

In a similar manner, Iran had to endure the prolonged years of the Taliban rule. The radical Sunni regime that waged a merciless war against Afghanistan's intricate tribal system and routinely massacred Afghan Shiites provided a formidable challenge for the Islamic Republic. In the summer of 1998, the killing of ten Iranian diplomats by Taliban forces in Mazar-i-Sharif nearly led the two states to go to war

---

23 Adam Tarock, "The Politics of the Pipeline: The Iran and Afghanistan Conflict," *Third World Quarterly* 20 (1999); Valerie Piacentini, "The Afghan Puzzle," *Iranian Journal of International Affairs* (Summer 1996); Olivier Roy, "The New Political Elite of Afghanistan," in *The Politics of Social Transformation in Afghanistan, Iran and Pakistan,* ed. Myron Weiner and Ali Bnuazizi (Syracuse: Syracuse University Press, 1994), 72–101.

against each other. Beyond active confrontation, Iran was extraordinarily alarmed by the puritanical Taliban regime's reliance on the drug trade and on Sunni terrorist organizations such as al Qaeda to sustain its power. Today, a large portion of Afghan drugs end up in Iran, creating its addiction crisis; it is estimated that the Islamic Republic may have as many as two million drug addicts. Given these realities, Iran soon emerged as the most durable foe of the Taliban. Indeed, despite the presence of U.S. forces in Afghanistan since 2001, the theocratic regime finds the existing configuration of power whereby Sunni militancy is largely tempered and a benign government reigns in Kabul an acceptable outcome.[24]

While Iran's relations with Afghanistan have improved over the years, its ties to Pakistan have at times been problematic. Pakistan's policy of using Afghanistan as a conduit for assertion of influence over Central Asia has greatly troubled Iran.[25] At a time when the Bush administration loudly proclaims Pakistan a valuable ally in its "war against terrorism," it conveniently neglects the fact that it was Islamabad that sustained the Taliban and tolerated its al Qaeda ally. The cynical Pakistani policy of unleashing the Taliban upon the hapless Afghan nation as a means of securing a bridge to Central Asia confronted Iran with a pronounced strategic threat. Since the fall of the Taliban, the relations between the two powers have markedly improved, as the issue of Afghanistan no longer divides them. However, Iran does remain concerned about internal stability of the Pakistani state, with its ample nuclear depositories. From Tehran's perspective, the prospect of a radical Sunni regime coming to power in Pakistan with its finger on the nuclear button is nearly an existential threat. As such, once more stability is the guide of Iran's policy toward yet another unpredictable neighbor.

It may come as a shock to the casual observer accustomed to U.S. officials' incendiary denunciations of Iran as a revisionist ideological power to learn that in various important regions, the Islamic Republic's

---

24 Barnett Rubin, "The Fragmentation of Afghanistan," *Foreign Affairs* (Winter 1989/1990); Barnett Rubin, "Post-Cold War State Disintegration: The Failure of International Conflict Resolution in Afghanistan," *Journal of International Affairs* (Winter 1993).

25 Hunter, *Iran and the World*, 130–138; Fuller, *The Center of the Universe*, 230–231.

policy has historically been conditioned by pragmatism. Today, Iran's approach to the Persian Gulf sheikdoms and its Eurasian neighbors is predicated on national-interest designs largely devoid of an Islamic content. The same cannot be asserted in the case of the Arab East, as the theocratic state's dogmatic opposition to the state of Israel has deprived its policy of the nuance and flexibility that has characterized its approach to many of its neighboring states. It is likely that this central contradiction in Iran's regional policy will persist, as Tehran may continue with its perplexing mixture of radicalism and moderation, pragmatism and defiance.

In the end, in formulating its regional vision, the Islamic Republic has sought to marry the two disparate strands of Iran's identity: Persian nationalism and Shiite Islam. As a great civilization with a keen sense of history, Iran has always perceived itself as the rightful leader of the Middle East. For centuries, Persian empires had dominated the political and cultural landscape of the region, inspiring a national narrative that views Iran's hegemony as both beneficial and benign. At the same time, as a persecuted religious minority, Shiites in Iran have always been suspicious and wary of their neighbors. The reality of rising Arab states, domineering Western empires, and Iran's religious exceptionalism has not ended Tehran's perception of itself as the "center of the universe," a society that should be emulated by the benighted Arab masses. Successive Persian monarchs and reigning mullahs would subscribe to this national self-perception, giving Tehran an inflated view of its historic importance.

A final important factor that has intruded itself uneasily in Iran's international orientation is pragmatism. Iran may perceive itself as uniquely aggrieved by the great powers' machinations, and it may nurse aspirations to emerge as the regional leader. However, the limitations of its resources and the reality of its actual power have sporadically led to reappraisal and retrenchment. The intriguing aspect of Iran's policy is that it can be both dogmatic and flexible at the same time. The Islamic Republic may take an ideologically uncompromising position toward Israel, yet deal pragmatically with its historic Russian nemesis. The tensions between Iran's ideals and interests, between its aspirations and limits, will continue to produce a foreign policy that is often inconsistent and contradictory.

2

The Need for a Comprehensive Approach to the Iran Nuclear Issue

Hitoshi Tanaka*

Since the 2002 revelation by Iranian dissidents that Tehran had begun secret construction of a uranium enrichment facility, few issues have attracted more concern in international security policy circles. Despite extensive efforts by the EU-3 (France, Germany, and the United Kingdom) and, more recently, the 3 plus 3 (also known as the P5 plus 1 group, comprising the United States, China, Russia, France, Great Britain, and Germany) to proactively engage Iran and convince its leaders to increase the transparency of its nuclear program, Iran's intransigence as well as its uranium enrichment activities continue.

A nuclear Iran would pose a grave threat to peace and stability in the Middle East and, by extension, to the security of global energy supplies. A nuclear Iran would also do irrevocable damage to the Nuclear Non-Proliferation Treaty (NPT), a regime already teetering on the verge of collapse, and threaten the continued effectiveness of global governance. Efforts thus far, which have essentially treated Iran's nuclear program as an isolated problem, have failed to achieve tangible progress. It is abundantly clear that concerned parties must reexamine the current approach and begin to work toward a comprehensive settlement that treats resolution of the nuclear issue as one aspect of a larger effort to create a more sound and stable security environment in the Middle East.

In light of this and also of the author's extensive experience dealing with the North Korean and Iranian nuclear issues, particularly in his past capacity as director-general of Asia and oceanic affairs in the Japanese Foreign Ministry (2001–2002) and deputy minister of foreign affairs (2002–2005), this paper will adopt a comparative approach and

---

* This paper was prepared with Adam P. Liff, research associate at the Japan Center for International Exchange (JCIE).

address the challenges posed by the nuclear programs of both Iran and North Korea.

Global Governance

The most salient obstacle to efforts to resolve the issues surrounding Iranian and North Korean nuclear proliferation is, ironically, the international community's inability to present a united front and deal with these nations in a consistent manner. Extant divisions within the international community on these issues are largely an outgrowth of the belligerent approach toward so-called rogue states adopted by the administration of U.S. President George W. Bush during his first term. A climate supportive of unilateralism in the aftermath of the September 11, 2001, terrorist attacks; the designation in President Bush's 2002 State of the Union address of Iraq, Iran, and North Korea as members of an "axis of evil"; and the articulation of the right to engage in preemptive war or preventive war, or both, codified in the 2002 "National Security Strategy of the United States" have all created the perception that the U.S. government pursues regime change over constructive engagement. This approach has dealt a serious blow to global governance.

Unfortunately, the U.S. decision to adopt a confrontational stance toward Iraq, Iran, and North Korea was largely predicated on intelligence analyses and assessments that ranged in reliability from tenuous to completely incorrect. The main rationale promulgated by the U.S. government to legitimate the 2003 invasion of Iraq—that is, the existence of weapons of mass destruction—was shown to be wrong after extensive searches following the overthrow of Saddam Hussein discovered no evidence of such weapons. Meanwhile, the administration's ongoing assertion that Iran is actively working to develop nuclear weapons runs counter to the U.S. intelligence community's 2007 National Intelligence Estimate (NIE), which concluded that Tehran halted its weapons program in 2003. Finally, the original intelligence assessment concerning North Korea's highly enriched uranium program, which was a primary factor behind the administration's decision to adopt a confrontational approach toward Pyongyang, has been gradually toned down during the course of the Six-Party Talks.

Many critics contend that in each of the aforementioned situations the Bush administration elected to adopt a unilateral and confrontational stance prior to formulating a sound plan for dealing with the consequences of such an approach. These critics argue that U.S. belligerence was at least partially responsible for the following developments: Pyongyang's decision to accelerate its nuclear weapons program and subsequently test a nuclear bomb in October 2006, the continuing instability in Iraq after more than five years of U.S. occupation, and the emergence of an increasingly powerful Iran widely suspected of pursuing regional hegemony in the absence of its traditional power balancer—Iraq. If the Bush administration had decided to proactively support comprehensive engagement (for example, back the efforts of the EU-3 to engage Iran in 2003) rather than attempt to contain and intimidate these troublesome regimes, current circumstances might have been avoidable.

It should be stressed that the objective of this chapter is not to dwell on such criticism but to argue that it is incumbent upon us to learn from past mistakes. It is not only the United States, but the entire international community, that bears responsibility for these errors. The developments discussed above elucidate why the international community must proactively engage Iran and North Korea and adopt a comprehensive approach to resolving problems surrounding their nuclear programs.

Good Cop, Bad Cop

In the immediate aftermath of the revelations that both Iran and North Korea had covertly restarted their nuclear programs, concerned parties adopted what could be considered a "good cop, bad cop" approach. European states and Japan played the role of the good cop, constructively engaging Iran and North Korea, while the United States adopted a role of bad cop, hoping that belligerent rhetoric and a confrontational line would succeed in convincing both regimes to abandon their nuclear programs.

Japan and North Korea

In the wake of the Bush administration's 2001 review of U.S. policy toward North Korea, Japanese leaders aimed to distance themselves from the U.S. administration's hard line and confrontational approach toward Pyongyang. Under Prime Minister Junichiro Koizumi, Japan worked assiduously to engage the North Korean regime, an effort that led to a summit meeting with Kim Jong-il in 2002. This historic event led to both the signing of the Pyongyang Declaration, a document that lays out a comprehensive road map for normalization of relations between Japan and North Korea, as well as the admission by Kim Jong-il that North Korean agents abducted Japanese citizens in the 1970s and 1980s.

Japan and Iran

Although the EU-3's constructive engagement policy vis-à-vis Iran has been extensively documented elsewhere, Japan's efforts to engage Iran are perhaps less widely understood. Although cooperation between Japan and the United States has expanded in a wide range of fields in recent years, Iran policy continues to be one area in which the allies continue to agree to disagree.

In contrast with the United States, which severed diplomatic relations with Tehran and banned all Iranian oil imports following the 1979 overthrow of the shah, Japan places a great deal of importance on maintaining stable ties with Iran. This is manifest in Japan's official development assistance policy; to date, Japan has provided more than ¥84 billion to Iran.[1] The two nations enjoy complementary trade relations: Iran is a major oil exporter, depending on oil revenues for 20 percent of its gross domestic product, and Japan is a major oil importer.[2] Japan-Iran bilateral trade levels reached $12.3 billion in 2006, dwarfing commerce between the United States and Iran ($243 million).[3] Iran is Japan's third-largest source of oil, and Japan is the largest consumer of Iranian oil.[4] Despite the collapse of talks over Japan's development of the Azadegan oil field in 2006, INPEX Holdings (Japan's energy exploratory firm)[5] still maintains a 10 percent stake in the project. Economic ties between Tokyo and Tehran continue to deepen, with Japan's purchases of Iranian oil on the rise, increasing by 27 percent between November 2006 and November 2007.[6]

------

1 "Islamic Republic of Iran—Statistics," Ministry of Foreign Affairs of Japan, www.mofa.go.jp/mofaj/area/iran/data.html.

2 Kenneth Katzman, *Iran: U.S. Concerns and Policy Responses* (Washington, D.C.: Congressional Research Service, May 6, 2008).

3 "Islamic Republic of Iran—Statistics"; "Trade with Iran: 2006," U.S. Census Bureau, www.census.gov/foreign-trade/balance/c5070. html#2006.

4 "Iran," U.S. Department of Energy, Energy Information Administration, www.eia.doe.gov/emeu/cabs/Iran/Oil.html.

5 Kamiguri Takashi and Abe Hideaki, "Japan's Iran Dilemma," Asia Times Online, January 31, 2006, www.atimes.com/atimes/Japan/ HA31Dh02.html.

Although the relationship between Japan and Iran is based primarily on commercial interests, several recent intergovernmental initiatives suggest policymakers from both countries may be looking to deepen bilateral ties. In addition to a steady stream of rhetoric suggesting future cooperation in energy security and collaborative programs to bring growth and prosperity to the Middle East, the two nations hold frequent political consultations at both the foreign minister and deputy foreign minister levels. Recent years have seen the emergence of bilateral dialogue on security issues, such as the consultation on disarmament and nonproliferation issues[7] as well as four rounds of human rights dialogue.[8] Although bilateral ties have undoubtedly diversified, it is nevertheless important to not overstate the significance of these initiatives, most of which have only just begun.

As far as the nuclear issue is concerned, Japan has been an active, if quiet, player. Japan has consistently expressed its concern about Iran's nuclear program in bilateral meetings and has worked assiduously to use its own experiences to convince Iran of the need to gain the trust of the international community prior to becoming a civilian nuclear power. In 2003, Japan utilized the Group of Eight framework to convince the Bush administration of the need for the EU-3 initiative to engage Iran. Japan has also played a role behind the scenes as a diplomatic bridge between Tehran and Washington. Japanese diplomats, for example, have frequently conveyed U.S. concerns to Iranian diplomats about Iran's support for Hezbollah and Hamas, the border issue with Iraq, and what Washington regards as Iranian efforts to sabotage the Middle East peace process. Japan has also served as a conduit for Iranian concerns. For example, Japanese diplomats have passed on Iranian leaders' immense frustration with Washington's insistence on treating Iran as an international pariah and Washington's unwillingness to regard Iran as a full-fledged and legitimate player in international affairs.

---

6 "Statistics," Japan Ministry of Economy, Trade, and Industry, www.meti. go.jp/english/statistics/downloadfiles/h2j581011e.pdf.

7 "Seventh Japan-Iran Consultation on Disarmament and Non-Proliferation Issues," Ministry of Foreign Affairs of Japan, July 6, 2007, www.mofa.go.jp/announce/event/2007/7/1174440_852.html.

8 "4th Japan-Iran Human Rights Dialogue," Ministry of Foreign Affairs of Japan, July 4, 2007, www.mofa.go.jp/announce/event/2007/7/1174393_852.html.

Nevertheless, Japanese diplomats have long understood that such tactics can be of only limited effectiveness and that a good cop, bad cop strategy is simply inapplicable to an issue like nuclear proliferation, which poses a clear and present danger to global peace and stability. The only way to resolve the manifold issues outstanding between Tehran and the international community is for the core nations to meet in both bilateral and multilateral contexts to address the nuclear issue in comprehensive terms. Lessons from the Six-Party Talks over North Korea's nuclear program can be instructive in this regard. It is also imperative that the international community recognize that the Iranian and North Korean nuclear issues are not merely issues of concern to their respective regions but are clear threats to the relevance of global governance for solving such problems.

The NPT Regime

Despite a substantial amount of cynicism about the prospects for success of the NPT at the time of its signing in 1968, the treaty has proved to be remarkably resilient during the past four decades. Although a number of member states have initiated nuclear weapons programs over the years (for example, Libya and South Africa), all but one state ultimately agreed to abandon its program. Despite this remarkable track record, recent developments such as North Korea's 2003 declaration of withdrawal from the NPT and subsequent nuclear weapons test, as well as Iran's history of covert nuclear programs and repeated violations of its treaty commitments, have brought the continued viability of the treaty into question. Failure to quickly and resolutely settle issues surrounding the nuclear programs of these two states could contribute greatly to the total collapse of the treaty regime and usher in an era of widespread nuclear proliferation. A brief discussion of North Korea and Iran's nuclear programs may prove instructive.

As far as damage to the NPT regime is concerned, North Korea's actions constitute a far more serious violation than those of Iran. Not only did Pyongyang repeatedly flout its commitments to the NPT throughout the 1990s, in 2003 it became the first—and, to date, only—state to announce its withdrawal from the treaty. Furthermore, it now declares itself to be a full-fledged nuclear power. Although its nuclear weapons remain technologically immature, North Korea's October 2006 nuclear test proved to the world that it has in fact succeeded in developing a functional nuclear bomb. If one takes the regime's rhetoric at face value, it would appear as though the international community's efforts to denuclearize the Korean peninsula are futile and that the world has no choice but to recognize and accept North Korea as a nuclear power.

In contrast with North Korea, which made it very clear that the goal of its nuclear program was the development of a weapon, Iran has not clarified the objectives of its program. Ever since Iran's covert nuclear program first came to light in 2002, Tehran has consistently argued that it maintains no designs for a weapons program and is merely seeking peaceful nuclear technology, a right it (correctly) argues is afforded to all signatories of the NPT. In negotiations with Japan, Iranian diplomats often point to Japan as a model of what Iran wishes to become: a peaceful state with the technology necessary to develop a full fuel cycle and an advanced civilian nuclear program. The Japanese have often pointed out, however, that Iran's history of violating its NPT obligations and conducting a clandestine military program have severely damaged the international community's confidence in the reliability of its claims.

In light of Iran's history of deception and ongoing refusal to cease uranium enrichment, it is perfectly natural that the international community remains skeptical of Tehran's assertion that it has no intention of developing nuclear weapons. At the same time, however, policymakers must not forget that there is in fact little, if any, hard evidence to indicate that Iran is merely prevaricating. On one hand, although an NIE released by the U.S. intelligence community late last year does acknowledge that Iran maintained a military nuclear program in the past, it also concludes that the program has been frozen since 2003. On the other hand, intentions are much less transparent than capabilities, and the international community must remain vigilant and ensure that Iran does not develop nuclear weapons.

The international community must learn several lessons from its experiences dealing with Iran and North Korea. First is the importance of formulating a list of clearly defined consequences for NPT violations so that potential violators are fully aware of the punishments they will face if they shirk their obligations. Second is the importance of diplomacy. Up to this point, the international community's approaches to dealing with the North Korean and Iranian nuclear programs have been ad hoc, inconsistent, and ineffective. Furthermore, they have offered potentially dangerous lessons to other states flirting with the idea of pursuing nuclear weapons. By sanctioning Iran for its rudimentary (and ostensibly peaceful) nuclear program and offering a comprehensive package of incentives (aid, oil, normalization of relations with Japan and the United States, among others) to induce North Korea to disband its nuclear weapons program, the international community has more or less announced to such states that their long-term interests would be better served by continuing to develop nuclear weapons and engaging the international community only after they have improved their negotiating position by becoming members of the nuclear club. For example, Iranian policymakers may look at North Korea's experience with the Six-Party Talks and calculate that the United States will treat Iran with respect only after it has become a nuclear power.

To ensure that Iran remains a faithful signatory of the NPT and does not follow North Korea's example, the international community must adopt a comprehensive approach that aims to address not only its own concerns about Iran's nuclear program but also the Iranian leaders' concerns, such as guaranteeing regime survival and normalizing relations with the United States.

Regional Security and Stability

In the case of North Korea and Iran, the dangers posed by nuclear weapons are exacerbated by the fact that both states exist in regions that are already rife with tension. The emergence of a new nuclear power in either of these regions, particularly in the case of Iran and the Middle East, could shift the balance of power sufficiently to catalyze conventional and nuclear arms races, with devastating consequences for both regional and global peace and stability.

Although both Iran and North Korea pose very real threats to the status quo in their respective regions, a nuclear Iran poses a significantly greater threat to global stability. Some might argue that North Korea's nuclear weapons have not significantly affected stability in Northeast Asia and assume that a nuclear Iran would therefore not have a substantial impact on peace in the Middle East, but such logic is fundamentally flawed. There are several reasons that a nuclear Iran would pose a much more egregious threat to stability in the Middle East than a nuclear North Korea poses in East Asia.

First and foremost, while all of North Korea's neighbors either have nuclear weapons themselves (China and Russia) or enjoy a nuclear umbrella provided by a third party (Japan and South Korea), the only existing (yet undeclared) nuclear power in the Middle East is

Israel. Consequently, a nuclear-armed Iran would almost surely create a domino effect and compel Saudi Arabia and others to seek nuclear deterrents for themselves.

Second, in terms of the traditional measures of national power (economic strength, population, military expenditures, for example), North Korea is by far the weakest nation in Northeast Asia. Nuclear weapons and nuclear umbrellas coupled with enormous conventional arsenals dwarfing North Korea's own leave Pyongyang's neighbors feeling relatively little immediate threat from a few rudimentary North Korean nuclear bombs. Iran, in contrast, is already the largest and most powerful state in the Middle East, particularly since the 2003 U.S. invasion of Iraq significantly enervated its historical nemesis. If Iran were to acquire nuclear weapons, it would exacerbate the power imbalance within the region and destabilize an already fragile peace.

Third, North Korea is primarily concerned with deterring the United States, which its leaders see as a hostile power, and it is highly improbable that North Korea would unilaterally initiate a conflict or use nuclear weapons outside of self-defense or desperation. Iran, in contrast, not only maintains deep-seated enmity toward Israel, a nation that Iranian President Mahmoud Ahmadinejad said in 2005 should be "wiped out from the map," but it also has very tense relations with most of its Sunni neighbors.

Energy Supplies—Oil and Gas

Although Japan's high dependence on Middle Eastern oil (86 percent) may make it an extreme case, it is not unique among nations in its dependence on energy imports from the region. Europe and the United States are other powers whose energy supplies would be severely disrupted in the event of conflict in the Middle East. Given this unfortunate reality, it is abundantly clear that a confrontational approach toward Iran, which would involve sanctions and provocative threats of military action, not only is unlikely to succeed in convincing Tehran to abandon its nuclear program but also runs counter to Western interests given the disruptive impact it is likely to have on global energy prices. For example, the more likely a military confrontation becomes between the United States and Iran, the more unstable energy markets will become and the higher the price of oil will rise. As an aside, it should also be noted that sanctions or boycotts of Iranian oil are unlikely to achieve desired results, as developing nations with increasing energy needs (in particular India and China) are likely to swoop in and purchase oil and gas interests in the absence of Western buyers.

The Way Forward: A Comprehensive Approach

Six years after it came to the world's attention that Iran was covertly pursuing nuclear weapons, Iran's nuclear program is still active despite international protest and several rounds of UN sanctions. The lack of any specific win-win solution for diplomats to hold up as a realistic goal in negotiations with Iran has thus far frustrated attempts to resolve the current impasse.

The limited success of negotiations up to this point has made it clear that Iran is determined to acquire nuclear know-how and is unlikely to yield to foreign pressure, even when faced with international sanctions and threats of targeted air strikes. The time has come for the international community to reexamine its approach to the issue. Henceforth, the question of Iran's nuclear program must no longer be treated in isolation but as part of a comprehensive settlement that leads to a mutually beneficial solution.

Lessons from North Korea

As far as international efforts to address North Korea's nuclear program are concerned, the immediate policy objective has been to ensure that Pyongyang neither produces further weapons nor sells or transfers technology and know-how to other nations; in addition Pyongyang should be urged to take beginning steps toward verifiable denuclearization. The Six-Party Talks have been designed as a quid pro quo framework that, rather than unilaterally demanding that North Korea abandon its nuclear weapons, aims instead to constructively address the concerns of both sides and create a win-win permanent solution. To this end, the six nations have agreed on a comprehensive approach that places the North Korean nuclear issue in a broader context and engages Pyongyang in dialogue over a permanent peace regime on the peninsula, lays the groundwork for normalization of diplomatic relations with both Japan and the United States, and sets the stage for future economic and energy cooperation.

As far as dealing with Iran is concerned, it is inevitable that Iran will become a strong regional power with or without nuclear weapons. The sooner the international community recognizes this reality and adjusts its policies away from containment and toward managing Iran's rise, the sooner it will be able to resolve the nuclear issue and bring stability to the region. Thus, the international community must engage Iran in a comprehensive dialogue similar in format to the Six-Party Talks. This dialogue must address both Iran's concerns and those of the international community and ensure that Iran becomes a stabilizing factor in the Middle East. Preventing civil war in Iraq, which will require the cooperation of the United States, Iran, and the rest of the international community, is yet another convincing reason to begin this process as soon as possible.

The United States as the Primary Actor
Although the leaders of both Iran and North Korea undoubtedly feel a great deal of resentment toward the United States and are determined to publicly show resilience in the face of repeated U.S. warnings, Iranian diplomats often sing a different tune behind closed doors. In negotiations with Japan, for instance, interlocutors from both Iran and North Korea have consistently articulated a strong desire to be recognized by the United States. In particular, Iranians often express frustration with U.S. insistence on treating them as a rogue state rather than a legitimate sovereign power, and they argue that it is this lack of respect that is the reason behind the U.S. refusal to diplomatically engage Iran.

Given how important U.S. recognition is to Iranian leaders, it is abundantly clear that no attempt to resolve the Iranian nuclear issue will succeed without the active and constructive participation of the United States. The international community must proactively work to convince Washington that the time for good cop, bad cop has passed and that the United States must not only be present at negotiations with Iran but also adopt a leadership role. The success or failure of efforts to resolve the Iranian nuclear issue will hinge primarily on the extent to which the international community succeeds in doing this and whether it is capable of presenting a united front under U.S. leadership.

An Expanded Role for Japan
Henceforth, Japan must be included as a participant in negotiations over Iran's nuclear weapons program. Particularly in light of Japan's cordial ties with all Middle Eastern nations, its strong and long-standing economic relations with Iran, and its experience as a civilian nuclear power (which, as mentioned above, Iranian leaders often cite as a

model for their own aspirations), Japan undoubtedly stands to make a substantive contribution to a comprehensive settlement.

The Nature of the Comprehensive Approach

The Iranian nuclear issue should be placed in the context of a larger dialogue on transforming the Middle East into a more stable and secure region. The first, and perhaps most important, step in this process will be for the international community to stop labeling Iran as a pariah state and recognize it as a powerful, legitimate, and fully sovereign nation. The second step will be to establish a forum for negotiations: a plenary of eight nations comprising Iran, the United States, the United Kingdom, France, Germany, Russia, China, and Japan. The third step will be for participants in these negotiations to define relevant issues and establish working groups to brainstorm frameworks for solutions. Working groups should address such issues as Iran's nuclear program (uranium enrichment, fuel cycle, ratification of the NPT's Additional Protocol, civilian nuclear technology, oversight, and verification, for example), normalization of relations between Iran and the United States, counterterrorism, stability in Iraq, and regionwide economic and security cooperation. The nations involved in each working group will vary by issue and, when necessary, could also be expanded to include nations outside the core eight. After each working group reaches a consensus over how to proceed, the eight-party format will continue to play an integral role supervising the implementation of these agreements.

Conclusion

To ensure that efforts to resolve the Iranian nuclear issue succeed in achieving a soft landing, concerned nations must adopt a pragmatic and comprehensive approach that aims to achieve mutually beneficial outcomes through multilateral negotiations. How the international community handles this issue will have serious implications for global governance, the future viability of the NPT, security of global energy supplies, and peace and stability in the Middle East. Although all nations have a responsibility to learn from past failures, the next president of the United States in particular must approach the Iranian nuclear issue from a broader perspective and treat it as a foreign policy priority during the next four years.

3

Of Trust and Security: The Challenge of Iran

Volker Perthes

Relevance of Iran and of Getting It Right

There are common reasons for Trilateral countries to take Iran and the development of relations with Iran seriously; and there are particular reasons for Europe, for the United States, and for Japan and East Asia, respectively. The nuclear issue is central, but it is not the only issue that makes Iran relevant and makes it necessary to develop a sound and ideally a common strategy on Iran. Getting Iran and our Iran policies right will be of enormous relevance for the future of the Middle East and our relations with that region, for arms control, and for global governance. For Europe, it is also a question of neighborhood relations and a test case for the European Union's Common Foreign and Security Policy (CFSP).

Future of the Middle East

Apart from the Arab-Israeli conflict, the future of Iran's relations with the international community and with its regional environment constitutes the main geopolitical challenge in the wider Middle Eastern region. The nuclear issue, that is, Iran's attempt to master and run a full nuclear fuel cycle that, according to the assessment of most observers, could eventually be used to acquire a military nuclear capacity, is in the center of this challenge, but it is not the only contentious issue between Iran and the international community. In a sense, the nuclear conflict epitomizes the difficulties of that relationship. Developments around this issue will to some degree determine the future shape of Middle Eastern security, particularly of the Persian Gulf region—a region that, because of its energy resources, will maintain highest importance for the national interest calculations of the United States and Europe as well as East and South Asia. Iran's nuclear program could lower the barriers to nuclear proliferation. It has an impact on the security perceptions and policies of other states in the region as well as on the standing of Europe and of the West in general in the wider Middle East. While regional leaders, particularly in the Gulf monarchies, will ask whether and how Western states will contribute to their security, popular discourse in the region may feature the theme of a new Western crusade against Muslim nations. Eventually, international and regional actors together will have to show whether they are able to establish a security architecture for the region that offers reasonable prospects for long-term stability, or whether volatility will be institutionalized, as it were, with the United States and probably other extraregional actors continuing to project military power into the Gulf and the Middle East to manipulate shifting regional coalitions and balances.

Iran, although unique in many respects, is not an isolated country. Given the confessional split between the Sunni and the Shiite (the majority and the minority confessions in Islam), many Sunnis look at (predominantly) Shiite Iran with some apprehension. Despite this divide, however, Iran is a central part of and a crucial player in the Muslim world. A military conflict between the United States and Iran or between a Western coalition and Iran would further increase feelings of victimization and anti-Westernism in many Muslim societies. A resolution of conflicts with Iran in a peaceful and constructive manner, however, could narrow the gap and also set a standard for the interaction between Western liberal countries and states where Islamist parties are in power.

Future of the Nuclear Nonproliferation Regime

If Iran were to acquire nuclear weapons, this would weaken and could eventually mean the end of the Nuclear Non-Proliferation Treaty (NPT). Should Iran thus succeed in exploiting the loopholes of the current safeguard regime (by hiding evidence from and limiting access to inspectors, among other things), major powers would probably lose confidence in the NPT and reduce support for the International Atomic Energy Agency (IAEA). Other rising powers could try to follow the Iranian example. The threat to the nonproliferation regime is also the main motive for the IAEA's efforts to not only resolve the crisis with Iran but also develop the instruments for dealing with such issues in the future. Although one might argue that Iran would eventually be a more responsible nuclear power than Pakistan, the impact of Iran acquiring a military nuclear capability would be much larger than that of Pakistan's acquisition of the bomb, simply because Iran is a member of the NPT. Pakistan and India never were members and thus did not have to leave the NPT.

The risk of regional proliferation would be higher in the Middle East than it is in South Asia. The realization by many international actors, however, of the inherent risks in Iran's nuclear program and its implications has also brought a number of new, constructive ideas to the table. Arguably, without the Iranian challenge, we would not today have a serious discussion about regional enrichment centers under IAEA supervision, multilateral joint ventures to produce nuclear fuel, or amendments to the NPT that would, for example, make the Additional Protocol (providing for more intrusive inspections) mandatory. And renowned U.S. strategists like Henry Kissinger and George Shultz would probably not have started a new debate about a world without nuclear arms.[1]

Global Governance
Our capability to resolve the Iranian nuclear issue in a peaceful way could also become an indicator of the West's ability to deal with the aspirations of emerging regional powers in general, as well as the capacity of such powers to deal with their ambitions in a constructive way. The outcome of the nuclear conflict with Iran may indeed give one initial, partial answer to whether the rising powers of the South can still be integrated into the current system of global governance. Certainly, international institutions will have to be adapted not only to accommodate the rise of China and India, but also to create new legitimacy for these institutions worldwide. The questions of how nations like Brazil, Indonesia, South Africa, Mexico, or Iran and others deal with that system could be crucial. The alternative to a consensual adaptation of the institutions of global governance could well be a situation where changes in the international balance of forces eventually break that system and conflict characterizes a world that is not only multipolar, but polarized in multiple ways.

Test for Europe
Iran has become a serious test case for the European Union and its CFSP. While the EU's diplomatic influence in the Middle East has been limited,

---

1 See George P. Shultz, William J. Perry, Henry A. Kissinger, and Sam Nunn, "A World Free of Nuclear Weapons," *Wall Street Journal*, January 4, 2007.

Europe has effectively taken the lead in trying to reach a diplomatic solution between Iran and the international community. With the EU-3 (France, Germany, and the United Kingdom) taking the initiative and EU foreign policy chief Javier Solana gradually taking the lead role, a new format of European foreign policy activity appeared. It began at a time when Europe was unhappy with U.S. unilateralism and its use of military force to change the situation in the Middle East. Europe had to prove that it was able to devise alternative means for dealing with foreign and security policy challenges rather than just criticizing or trying to balance and block ill-fated U.S. policies and thereby become polarized internally. The EU-3 format initially created some uneasiness among smaller EU states even though they generally agreed with the content and aim of the initiative. The procedure, having three big members of the EU speak for the European Union, became more acceptable once Solana was associated with it.

For the EU, success in these international diplomatic efforts is also important to its own development as an actor in the international system. While failure and success are not clearly defined here, the breakdown of the diplomatic process or a nuclear breakout of Iran would increase skepticism with regard to the ability of the EU to deal with international threats. So far, Europe has grown with the challenge. It has developed its instruments and has been engaging in a robust diplomacy (involving not only a package of incentives but also sanctions and efforts to coordinate an international sanctions policy) in a multilateral process and a multilevel game. One can well describe the situation as playing chess with the Iranians, who sometimes exchanged their players rather than moved their figures, and poker with the United States, Russia, and China at the same time.

Transatlantic Relationship

The U.S. administration gradually accepted and then partially adopted the European approach and analysis. This pertained particularly to the assumption that Iran would react to external incentives and disincentives and that in order to influence the Iranian leadership one would have to take legitimate Iranian interests into consideration. Even though the U.S. leadership has not taken the military option off the table, this may be one of the very few recent cases where European policymakers managed to convince their partners in the United States (not all of them, certainly) of their approach, also creating some trust on the other side of the Atlantic that the Europeans might actually do (and not only see) some things right. It was also important that the EU managed to associate Russia and China with that approach, thereby giving way to the so-called 3 plus 3 format (France, Germany, and the United Kingdom plus the United States, Russia, China), a grouping that now regularly consults about its Iran policy and coordinates initiatives toward Iran as well as Security Council action. European diplomacy also played a crucial role in bringing countries like India and South Africa into that common approach, in the IAEA board of governors, or in the Security Council.

The management of the Iranian file is also a test for the transatlantic relationship as such. Should the diplomatic process break down, Iran could (again) cause a rift between EU countries and the United States. For European policymakers as well as European business, interaction with and policies toward Iran will never be handled without taking into consideration the state of relations with the United States and the question of how Washington may react to Europe's dealings with Tehran. It is essential from a European perspective, however, that such close coordination with Washington will not create an automatism whereby Europe in the end would be forced upon a U.S.-designed path of action that it never wanted to take.

Europe's Energy

Beyond the implications for regional security, and even beyond the special importance of the Middle East and the Persian Gulf region for global oil supply, Iran has a particular importance for Europe's energy security, not least so with regard to the chances of Europe to diversify its gas supplies. Iran and Qatar form the region with the largest natural gas reserves worldwide. Will this region eventually be connected to the region with the largest consumer demand for natural gas? Ideally, Iranian gas fields could be directly linked by pipeline to households all over Europe. This, however, depends not only on infrastructure laid through Turkey into the Middle East (the Nabucco project), but primarily on political developments in Iran and on the relationship between Iran and Europe. Iran is the most important state in Europe's wider Middle Eastern neighborhood, a country with not only natural resources but also enormous human resources and a rich and old civilization. Iran will also become a direct neighbor of the EU if Turkey should acquire a full or even a limited membership status in the EU. In the long run, not only a benign but probably a strategic, partnership could be envisioned between the EU and Iran. Doubtless, there is a long way to go before European-Iranian relations can be developed that far.

On What It Depends

A negotiated resolution of the nuclear conflict with Iran will depend on three variables. First, it will depend on an international consensus that Iran—or others outside the current circle of nuclear-armed states—must not be allowed to acquire nuclear weapons. Second, it will depend on the ability and willingness of the United States and Europe to communicate to Iran and to others that the contentious issue is proliferation, not the nature of the regime in Iran. And third, it will depend on domestic politics in Iran.

Particularly with regard to this third variable, we also have to realize that the political options of the West in general, and of Europe in particular, depend to a large extent on our analysis—on the understanding that we develop of the objects and partners of our policies. This includes the theoretical frames or the filters through which we tend to view the reality around us. If international politics are basically understood as a zero-sum game, and if Iran is simply seen as a state ruled by evil forces who have no other aim but to acquire nuclear arms to threaten and destroy others or at least enforce their hegemony on the Middle East, the range of policy options is rather limited. If we make an effort to enrich our analysis to a higher degree, however, by looking at the inside life, political divisions, conflicting interests, and historically and culturally transmitted norms and contexts of reasoning that have an influence on foreign policy or security policy decisions in Iran, our spectrum of available policy options increases.

Consequently, the success of our interaction with Iran regarding the nuclear issue as well as other problems is contingent on our ability to "read" Iran right. Are our instruments of analysis appropriate? Is the Islamic Republic of Iran an exceptional regime as concepts such as the "mullah regime" or "theocracy" suggest? Such concepts also presuppose that the leading actors in Iran are driven not by rational interest, but by some form of religious zeal or messianism. Or is Iran another semiauthoritarian postrevolutionary regime in a specific neighborhood whose actors are in the end driven by rational interest calculations? This is what Europeans in their dealings with Iran have generally been assuming, and it is also part of the analysis of the 2007 U.S. National Intelligence Estimate (NIE) on Iran. It implies that the Iranian leadership would react to incentives and disincentives and follow cost-benefit analysis, as other state actors do. The question of what drives Iranian policies is essential to the discussion about a sound international approach toward Iran. And it will therefore also assume a central place in this paper.

Historical Background

Analysts differ as to what drives the policies of the Islamic Republic of Iran, particularly with regard to its international relations. Most analysts agree that national interest has to be considered one or the main factor. But national interest is eventually what the political elite define as such. Different factors may be valued differently by different elite segments. So should we primarily try to understand security considerations, both with respect to territorial integrity and regime security, or rather the quest for regional leadership or hegemony?[2] Should we consider Islamic revolutionary motives, and the peculiarity of Iran being the only Shiite power, nationalism, domestic factional struggles,[3] or the search for economic chances as driving forces? The answer is all of these to varying degrees. And we also have to give consideration to the historical background.

Revolution, Reform, Pragmatism

Since the overthrow of the shah in January 1979, we can roughly distinguish three phases in the historical development of contemporary Iran—and a fourth one that is still ongoing. Each of these phases has shaped Iran's relations with its international environment in particular ways.

The first ten years are those of revolution and war. They are marked, initially, by the chaos of the revolution and the struggle for dominance after the fall of the old regime and the formation of the Islamic Republic with its very distinct constitutional shape. Not only because of the strong support of the United States for the shah's regime have the new leaders held strong anti-Western and particularly anti-U.S. feelings. The takeover of the U.S. embassy and the taking of its staff as hostages by

---

2 Shahram Chubin, *Iran's Nuclear Ambitions* (Washington, D.C.: Carnegie Endowment for International Peace, 2006).

3 Anoushiravan Ehteshami and Mahjoob Zweiri, *Iran and the Rise of Its Neoconservatives: The Politics of Tehran's Silent Revolution* (London: I. B. Taurus, 2007).

revolutionary students in 1979 therefore become a defining moment for the course of the new regime. The charismatic leader of the revolution, Ayatollah Ruhollah Khomeini, endorsed the act, which radical elements in the regime have since seen as a "second revolution." It is not only a breach of international norms but also a signal for a more radical domestic path and the ouster of more liberal forces who had supported the overthrow of the shah but were opposed to theocratic ideas such as the principle of *velayat-e faqih* (the rule of the jurist, that is, of the *rahbar* or spiritual leader) now ingrained into the constitution that was ratified by popular referendum in the midst of the crisis.

The new regime established its authority with revolutionary brutality. It frightened its neighbors with its radical rhetoric and more or less overt attempts to export the revolution into their lands. As a result, the regime was in domestic disarray and internationally isolated when it was attacked by Iraq's forces in the summer of 1980. The eight years of war that ensued incurred an enormous price in terms of human life (approximately 300,000 dead and 750,000 wounded) and material damage, but they also stabilized the regime. The war allowed the conservative core to strengthen its hold over the means of state power, to rigorously repress any opposition, and eventually to gain a rather broad legitimacy simply because the country was able to withstand an enemy that was not only supported by most Arab states but also by the United States. For many Iranians, particularly of the war generation, the main lesson of the war was that Iran will always have to rely on itself and that the United States, as well as other international powers, can never be trusted.

Khomeini died in mid-1989, one year after the end of the war. Ayatollah Ali Khamene'i, despite some doubts regarding his theological qualifications, was appointed as Khomeini's successor. Akbar Hashemi Rafsanjani, a midlevel cleric (*hojjatolislam*), businessman, and member of the inner circle around Khomeini, was elected president. The two presidential terms of Rafsanjani (1989–1997) are often referred to as the era of reconstruction. Rafsanjani tried to steer a pragmatic course, and economic recovery had priority. The government set out to improve Iran's relations with the rest of the world, particularly with the Arab Gulf states and with European countries. Europe and Iran started to engage in what initially was called a "critical dialogue" and later pursued as "conditioned engagement."[4] These attempts to reintegrate Iran into the

---

4 Johannes Reissner, "Europe and Iran: Critical Dialogue," In *Honey and*

international community were undermined by actions of the regime itself or of elements within the regime's security apparatus, resulting in the murders of Iranian opposition politicians in Germany that again severely strained relations with European countries. It was also under the Rafsanjani presidency that Iran restarted the nuclear program that Khomeini had discontinued after the revolution. Although Rafsanjani failed to liberalize the economy and to open the country to foreign direct investment, trade and consumption picked up, largely, however, at the expense of increasing foreign debt. Corruption also increased, and Rafsanjani left office rather unpopular.

The Rafsanjani era was also marked by some relaxation in the sociocultural and political atmosphere. Without that, the outcome of the 1997 presidential election would hardly have been possible. The candidate of the establishment lost, and Muhammad Khatami, a former minister of culture and a known reformist, was elected, mainly on the votes of the young and the female parts of the population. The two presidential terms of Khatami (1997–2005) can rightly be dubbed the era of reform despite the fact that the limits of political change left many of his supporters disappointed in the end. Under Khatami, Iran opened up culturally and intellectually. The president advocated a strong civil society, the rule of law, and the value of dialogue and democracy. In spite of remaining constraints, the political debate became lively; thousands of NGOs, independent publishing houses, and cultural initiatives emerged; universities acquired more independence; and political participation was encouraged.[5] Among other things, municipal elections were introduced (and became a measure for the general political mood).

Khatami was nonetheless often chided for his lack of resolve to push for wider political liberalization or even to defend liberal and democratic activists against the repression by the conservative and hard-line elements of the regime. In fact, he never had uncontested power. Although the reformists managed to gain a convincing electoral victory in the parliamentary elections of 2000, their ability to pursue their program was often limited through the power of other institutions

---

Vinegar: Incentives, Sanctions, and Foreign Policy, ed. Richard N. Haass and Meghan L. O'Sullivan (Washington, D.C.: Brookings Institution Press, 2000), 33–50.

5 For details, see Volker Perthes, *Orientalische Promenaden: Der Nahe und Mittlere Osten im Umbruch* (Munich: Siedler, 2006), 311–393.

firmly in the hands of conservative elements. The judiciary, the Guardian Council, and not least the *rahbar* blocked more than one reform project, and proreform media and journalists were often harassed. In the run-up to the 2004 parliamentary elections, the Guardian Council disqualified many reformist candidates. Liberal Iranian observers interviewed at that time spoke of a "parliamentary coup d'état by the Guardian Council." The reformists lost the parliamentary elections of 2004, but their loss was not only because of such interference. In fact, they had already lost the municipal elections one year earlier without any manipulation to their disadvantage. Although Khatami remained popular to the end of his second term, that was not necessarily so for his government, which was blamed for a lack of economic progress. The general mood turned to the conservatives, whose candidates for Parliament successfully presented themselves as more down to earth and better prepared to work on the economy and public services than the lofty intellectuals around Khatami. Their candidate list name, *Abadgeran* (developers), seemed programmatic.

Khatami's policy of dialogue was directed toward the international environment as well as toward his own populace. Relations with the Arab neighbors and with Europe improved, and the Khatami government also made some efforts to achieve a rapprochement with Washington. For a while, Iran's practical cooperation with the United States on Afghanistan after the fall of the Taliban seemed to introduce a more constructive bilateral relationship. The opening did not last long. In his State of the Union address in January 2002, President George W. Bush referred to Iran as part of an "axis of evil."[6] This strained the relationship again and also undermined Khatami domestically. The U.S. invasion of Iraq removed an archenemy of Iran but also brought U.S. military power worryingly close to Iranian territory. Beginning in the fall of 2003, the nuclear file became the main issue defining Iran's relationship with Western powers. It was unresolved when Khatami's second term ended (the constitution does not allow a president to serve for more than two terms in a row) and Mahmoud Ahmadinejad took over.

The end of the Khatami presidency also marked the end of the reform phase. The reformists lost in the first round of the presidential elections of summer 2005. None of the reformist candidates had the

---

6 "President Delivers State of the Union Address," White House, January 29, 2002, www.whitehouse.gov/news/releases/2002/01/20020129-11. html.

mobilizing appeal of Khatami, the reformist vote was split between two candidates, and voter turnout was low compared with previous elections. In the second round, Hashemi Rafsanjani, the conservative pragmatist who was then trying to make a comeback as president and who had emerged with a small lead in the first round, stood against the hard-line conservative and mayor of Tehran, Mahmoud Ahmadinejad. Ahmadinejad's victory resembled that of Khatami eight years before in that he also ran against the establishment candidate.

Ahmadinejad successfully played the role of the man of the people—uncorrupted—which set him off from Rafsanjani, and he appeared to be seriously interested in social justice and in the fate of the poorer part of the population to whom he promised jobs, improved public services, and better income. Although there was manipulation in the first round (the Guardian Council had disqualified all but seven candidates), Ahmadinejad's victory was real. He scored 17 million votes against 10 million for Rafsanjani. There were many factors that contributed to this success: popular disaffection with the reformists and their meager achievements, a class and antiestablishment effect, a skillful exploitation of nationalist feelings, and support from hard-liners within the institutions, including from the spiritual leader, Ayatollah Khamene'i.[7]

With Ahmadinejad's election, the Islamic Republic has certainly entered into a fourth phase of its political development. It is too early to tell how we eventually will have to characterize it. Although rather closely connected to the faction then called the *Abadgeran,* the loosely knit bloc of conservative parliamentarians, Ahmadinejad and his political camp call themselves *Osulgarayan* (principalists or fundamentalists). They are also often referred to as "neoconservatives," even by intellectuals close to the president's camp in a somewhat mocking self-comparison with U.S. neocons. The era of the new president may well be the phase of conservative backlash and external confrontation. Ahmadinejad not only speeds up the nuclear program and defies international demands and Security Council resolutions; he also raises deep suspicions about the intentions of Iran with his public reiteration of a Khomeini quote about Israel's disappearance from the annals of history and his repeated denial or questioning of the Holocaust. Relations have soured with the regional and international environment, and particularly with the West,

---

7 Ali M. Ansari, "Iran under Ahmadinejad: The Politics of Confrontation," *Adelphi Papers* 47, no. 393 (2007): 23–39.

and political and cultural freedoms in Iran have come under increasing attack. At the end of 2006, UN Security Council sanctions were imposed on the Islamic Republic for the first time; more sanctions followed in March 2007 and March 2008.

It is too early to tell how long this phase will last. Domestic criticism of Ahmadinejad has mounted, particularly for his lack of achievement on the economic front but also from Iran's politicized students for his antiliberalism. His political camp suffered heavy losses at the municipal elections and the elections to the Assembly of Experts in December 2006. While large parts of the political elite were wary about Ahmadinejad's confrontational foreign policy and extremely unhappy about the referral of the nuclear issue to the Security Council, the president managed to use the imposition of sanctions to mobilize his supporters and get the elite to close ranks, on the surface at least. If some elite members had talked about a possible impeachment of the president immediately after the municipal and Assembly of Experts elections in mid-December, such discussions were off as soon as, less than two weeks later, the first sanctions resolution was passed in the Security Council.

It is interesting that the release of the U.S. National Intelligence Estimate on Iran in November 2007,[8] which was widely seen as taking the option of an U.S. military attack on Iran off the table at least for the remainder of the Bush administration's term, had the opposite effect: it triggered anew a highly critical domestic debate about the performance of the government and particularly about Ahmadinejad's economic policies. The apparent removal of an external threat allowed internal criticism to mount. Even the spiritual leader, Ayatollah Khamene'i, showed his unhappiness with some of the president's moves, particularly with his apparent attempts to concentrate more power in his hands. In a quite unusual move, Khamene'i responded to complaints from Parliament and clarified that all "branches of power," that is, the president too, were bound by legislation that had gone through the constitutional procedures.[9]

Many Iranian observers therefore initially expected that the parliamentary elections of March 2008 would lead to a heavy defeat of

8 "Iran: Nuclear Intentions and Capabilities," National Intelligence Estimate (Washington, D.C.: Office of the Director of National Intelligence, November 2007), www.dni.gov/press_releases/20071203_release.pdf.

9 Nazila Fathi, "Iran Leader Backs Parliament in a Dispute with Ahmadinejad," *New York Times,* January 22, 2008.

the president and his political camp and a success for reformists and pragmatists around the two former presidents, Khatami and Rafsanjani. This did not take place. The Guardian Council disqualified an enormous number of candidates. Reformists of the Khatami camp, whose candidates, particularly their more prominent representatives, had been the main victims of these disqualifications, protested that the Guardian Council's vetting process had in effect become a "first round" of the elections that left little for voters to decide. In fact, the "Friends of Khatami" could eventually field candidates for only about one-third of the 290 seats, and the more centrist party of former reformist *majlis* speaker Mahdi Kharrubi for about half of them.

Ahmadinejad's faction, however, was not totally successful. The conservative camp was split between the president's Islamo-nationalist trend and the more pragmatic conservatives around the former secretary of the National Security Council, Ali Larijani; Tehran mayor Bagher Qalibaf; and former head of the Revolutionary Guards, Mohsen Reza'i, who, like the president and his friends, all define themselves as "principalists," denoting faithfulness to the principles of the Islamic revolution. They differ with Ahmadinejad on issues like the president's style of management, his economic policies, and also the way of handling the relationship with the international community, and they made these differences clear in the campaign. To some extent the elections became a contest, therefore, about leadership in the conservative camp and a first test for the presidential elections of 2009, where Ahmadinejad will certainly try to gain a second mandate while Larijani, Qalibaf, and Reza'i are seen as potential contenders. This race remains open.

In the parliamentary elections, Ahmadinejad's so-called United Principalist Front won the largest slice with close to 120 of the 290 seats; Larijani's Broad Principalist Front may have gathered some 75 or around one-quarter, and the two reformist candidate lists together somewhat more than 40 seats.[10] Ahmadinejad thus has no control over the *majlis*, but there is a strong conservative dominance and, with a partly overlapping and partly different membership, a pragmatic majority, too. Politically, the only clear winner was the spiritual leader, Khamene'i: his loyalists hold a majority, and the president has been reined in a bit.

---

10 Since the names of many candidates have been put on different lists and a substantial number of deputies have been elected as independents, some deputies will show their allegiance to only one faction or another once the *majlis* has begun its work. It is therefore impossible to give precise figures about the strength of individual groups in the *majlis*.

Power Structure and Power Struggle

Although it makes sense to distinguish the war and postwar phases of Iran with respect to the three presidents—Ali Khamene'i, Akbar Hashemi Rafsanjani, and Mohammed Khatami—the president does not shape the political path of the country. The Islamic Republic of Iran is not simply another authoritarian system. Rather, it is hybrid in more than one sense: it combines republican and theocratic, democratic and authoritarian or despotic, or, as some analysts would stress, modern and traditional elements (see Figure 1). The tradition, however, is clearly "invented": the history of Islam knows the caliphate, the direct rule by the successor (caliph) of the Prophet, and the absolutist rule of the sultan, or *amir al-mu'minin* (commander of the faithful). The *velayat-e faqih,* the rule or authority of the jurisprudent, is an invention by Khomeini. It institutionalizes control by the spiritual (or supreme) leader over the government and all other institutions so as to make the state, its laws, and practices conform to God's will. While making the postrevolutionary state a republic, Khomeini's constitution also introduces modern institutions and procedures, such as regular elections and court appeals. The result is a complex system with competing authorities and theocratic as well as republican power centers.

The spiritual leader (*rahbar*) holds the strongest position, but given the other elements—republican and democratic—in the system, the leader is not a dictator. He only supervises political life; however, he can block or undo decisions of the Parliament and of the government, and he appoints the heads of and controls the security apparatus, the judiciary, the media, and the religious foundations (*bonyads*). This gives him enormous worldly influence and patronage. A network of personal representatives in all important institutions and agencies helps him to stay informed and exercise direct influence.[11] The Leader is elected, for lifetime, by the Assembly of Experts, a council of clerics that in turn is elected by universal suffrage every eight years. Theoretically at least, the Experts Assembly has the power to dismiss and replace the spiritual leader.

The main republican elements in the constitutional setup are the Parliament and the president, both elected by universal suffrage. Parliament, aside from its legislative function, could impeach the president

---

11 On Khamene'i, his background, and his thinking see Karim Sadjadpour, *Reading Khamenei: The World View of Iran's Most Powerful Leader* (Washington, D.C.: Carnegie Endowment for International Peace, 2008).

Figure 1: Organization of the Government of Iran

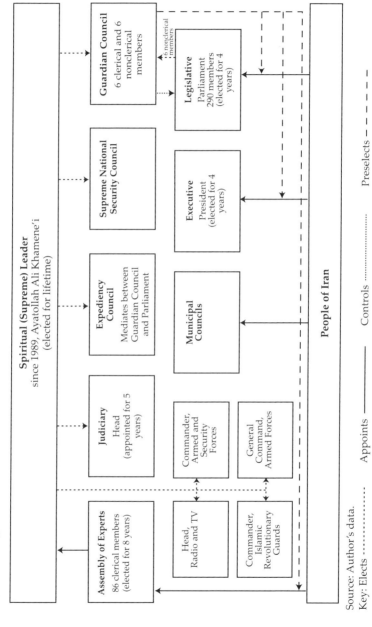

Source: Author's data.

Key: Elects ············· Appoints ——— Controls ············· Preselects – – –

with a two-thirds majority and the consent of the spiritual leader. The president appoints the cabinet, but cabinet members need to obtain a vote of confidence in Parliament. The president also appoints the members of the Supreme National Security Council (SNSC), though the supreme leader has at least one representative on the SNSC.

Another central institution on the theocratic side of the structure is the Guardian Council. It is composed of twelve jurists, half of them clerics chosen by the Leader, the other half chosen by Parliament. The Guardian Council interprets the constitution, supervises elections, and approves or disqualifies candidates for the Experts Assembly, the presidency, and Parliament. It also has functions akin to a constitutional court, vetting (and often rejecting) laws. An increasingly influential body is the so-called Expediency Council (precisely translated as Council for the Determination of the Interests of the System). Its members are appointed by the spiritual leader; its main function is to mediate between the Guardian Council and Parliament.

Other institutions also have an influence on decisions. This is certainly the case for the SNSC, for the judiciary, for the Pasdaran (the Revolutionary Guard) that practically is a parallel military structure that controls vast economic interests, and for the *bonyads* (religious foundations) that are in all but name big business consortia under the control of the clergy. Finally, there is the clergy itself: Qom, the center of religious learning, and the currently eight grand ayatollahs have been largely sidelined but still enjoy legitimacy and some authority.

The system gives the spiritual leader the authority as supreme arbiter and prime decision maker on major political issues. For affairs not directly dealt with by the leader, the system provides a host of checks and balances. This gives expression to the intraelite pluralism of the Islamic Republic, and it gives the system both flexibility and stability in the sense that it can manage political crises and rejuvenation within the elite.

The fact is, however, that all centers of power can, to one extent or another, also act as veto players and block or put a brake on decisions. The system seems to be characterized by an institutionalized permanent struggle for preeminence, a "war of positions,"[12] among the various centers of power. As a result, it is often not clear who is really in charge—unless the leader himself decides. In the foreign policy

---

12 Jean-Pierre Perrin, "Ahmadinejad: le début de la fin?" *Politique internationale* 115 (2007): 52.

field, for example, a host of institutions could legitimately claim a say, if not the say, over policies: the president, the foreign minister, the Parliament, but also the SNSC and its secretary, as well as a Strategic Council for Foreign Relations that was set up as recently as 2006. It is composed of former foreign ministers and is supposed to advise the spiritual leader on international and foreign policy questions. It may not have any real power, but because it was established as the crisis between Iran and the international community deepened, many local observers saw it as an attempt by Khamene'i to balance the president's dangerous foreign policy moves.

The system is certainly not democratic in a liberal sense, but it is not just another Middle Eastern autocracy. To an extent, the regime is accountable to the people, and participation rates in elections—some 60 percent in the 2005 presidential elections as well as the 2008 parliamentary elections—suggest that the institutions enjoy some legitimacy, or at least that people take them seriously. Election outcomes have also not been predictable as in more closely controlled systems. Voters use elections to express their dissatisfaction with those in charge. This was clearly the case with the municipal and Experts Assembly elections of December 2006,[13] as well as the June 2005 presidential elections. Previously, in 1997, Khatami was elected against everybody's expectations.

Public opinion in Iran is somewhat difficult to gauge. Anecdotal evidence as well as somewhat dubious polls[14] suggest, not very surprisingly, that the economy has become Iranians' top priority. In their electoral programs or pamphlets, almost all candidate lists and individual candidates running for the 2008 elections gave priority to themes like inflation, unemployment, or rising rents. In contrast, the majority of Iranians does not seem to be particularly interested in Iran's support for Hezbollah or for the Palestinians, or in picking a fight with Israel. There is sympathy with the Palestinians but also a general feeling that the well-being and the interests of one's own country should come first. The perception that Iranian people are poor because the regime was "throwing all that money at the Palestinians and the Lebanese" is certainly incorrect, but this author has been confronted with it more

---

13 Johannes Reissner, "Iran: Wahlschlappe und Sanktionen," *SWP-Aktuell* (January 2007).

14 See, for example, "Khomeini's Children," *The Economist*, Supplement: Special Report on Iran, July 21, 2007.

than once when speaking to Iranians not connected to the elite.[15] As oil income was visibly increasing and Ahmadinejad had promised to create jobs and improve the life of the poorer parts of the population, the disappointing economic performance became his weak point, much as the economy is the weak point of the Islamic Republic in general.

Iran's Economy: Waiting to Be Kicked Alive

Given its resource endowment, Iran could easily be one of the emerging economies of the South, a possible member of the next generation of BRICs (Brazil, Russia, India, and China). But it is not. It can rightly be called "industrializing," but it has been in this state since the era of the shah. Some new production facilities have been set up, particularly automotive industries, a sector where Iran has advanced from only assembling foreign-brand cars to designing and producing its own passenger car, the Samand, with mainly domestic input. Iran also produces some high-tech industrial goods such as turbines for power stations, but it still has some way to go to becoming an industrial country. According to a vision paper that predicted Iran in 2024 that was prepared under the Khatami government and approved by the leader in 2003—sometimes referred to as a twenty-year plan—Iran is supposed to increase non-oil exports. The implicit aim of deriving more income from industrial production than from hydrocarbon exports seems rather unrealistic for some time to come. The vision paper is also the basis for the plan to eventually generate 20,000 megawatts from fifteen to twenty nuclear power stations.

Iran has the largest oil and gas reserves worldwide after Saudi Arabia and Russia. Oil and gas make up over 80 percent of all exports, more than 50 percent of budget income, and up to 30 percent of GDP. But the hydrocarbon sector is not in good shape. Much of the infrastructure is old and run down. By 2007, Iran produced some 3.8 million barrels per day of oil and exported about 2.4 million barrels per day. As local demand rises with growing motorization, Iran needs to increase its production—or, indeed, generate energy from other sources—if it wants to maintain its export levels. Because of the lack of refinery capacity, Iran already has to import close to 100,000 barrels per day, which is about 40 percent of its local petrol consumption. Subsidies for petrol

---

15 See also Karim Sadjadpour, "How Relevant Is the Iranian Street?" *Washington Quarterly* 30, no. 1 (2006): 154.

imports are estimated to cost the state up to $5 billion per year. In the summer of 2007, petrol was rationed for the first time.

To increase oil production and build up proper refinery capacity, foreign technology and probably foreign investment will be needed.[16] Overall investment needs in the oil and gas sector are estimated at between $100 and $150 billion over the next five to seven years.[17] But investor-unfriendly attitudes and opaque rules in the Iranian bureaucracy, the general political insecurity, as well as international sanctions have scared away many potential investors, particularly from Western countries.

Chinese, Indian, Malaysian, or Turkish companies are less deterred though. Among other things, Chinese companies are involved in the expansion of the pipeline system that brings Central Asian oil to northern Iran (to be swapped for Iranian oil being exported through the Persian Gulf); Sinopec concluded a $2 billion deal on developing the Yadavaran oil field in December 2007; and the China National Offshore Oil Corporation had signed a deal to develop the North Pars gas field one year earlier. Turkey and Iran signed a memorandum of understanding in mid-2007 about the development of parts of the South Pars gas field by Turkish companies and the eventual transport of Iranian gas to Europe via Turkey.

Up to 80 percent of Iran's GDP is produced by state-owned companies or parastatals—mainly the *bonyads,* revolutionary religious foundations that, in effect, have become major business corporations and patronage networks under the control of influential members of the clerical establishment. Ayatollah Khamene'i and the government have publicly committed themselves to privatization both through the sale of government companies to the private sector and by rescinding investment restrictions that have hitherto reserved certain industries for state or semistate companies. Privatization is foreseen in the constitution of the Islamic Republic, and it is in line with the conservative, but

---

16 According to Iran's oil minister, Vaziri Hamoneh, the output of Iran's oil fields will fall by 13 percent a year if new investments cannot be made; see *Strategic Survey 2007* (London: International Institute for Strategic Studies, 2007), 223.

17 This estimate was offered by the deputy oil minister and a study by the Center for Strategic Research and was reported in *Tehran Times International,* February 3, 2008. In international reports, figures vary greatly. For even higher estimates, see Jean-Pierre Perrin, "Ahmadinejad: le début de la fin?" *Politique internationale* 115 (2007): 59.

market friendly, attitude of the ruling stratum. Most of the regime elite see privatization as unavoidable in order to modernize the economy and make Iranian companies more competitive.

Progress, however, has been slow. Also, as in so many transforming economies, the rationale of privatization is undermined by fears of losing control. At least a small group in the government believes that the more powerful the private sector becomes, the more it will interfere in politics. And powerful segments in the bureaucracy and the *bonyads* do not want to give up the patronage, particularly the ability to provide jobs that comes with the control of large swatches of the economy. As long as the government seeks to maintain its say over the appointment of the management through minority shares, however, or through the transfer of shares to state-controlled banks or insurance companies, the interest of the private sector to respond to the public offerings of these companies' stocks remains limited. It is more likely that the private sector will be strengthened by its move into previously restricted areas such as upstream and downstream investments in the oil industry or telecommunications. A number of private banks and investment companies have already been established.[18]

Iran's population of 71 million, about twice as many as at the time of the revolution in 1979, is highly urbanized and young (70 percent live in the cities, two-thirds are under thirty years of age), and it is relatively well educated, certainly in regional comparison. Literacy is almost universal. This population would provide the human basis for an economic takeoff. With few investments, however, many do not find qualified jobs. Unemployment is estimated at 15 percent. Many graduates try to find work abroad. Even Iranian money is invested in Dubai rather than in Iran: 400,000 Iranians are living in the emirate on the other side of the Persian Gulf, and approximately sixteen daily flights to Dubai enable Iranians to see and experience how money and an investment-friendly climate can create sprawling growth in contrast with the picture in their own country.

When Ahmadinejad was elected, he promised to bring oil revenues to every family, diminish poverty, and tackle unemployment. Despite the steep rise in oil prices, however, the president has not done well on the economic front. Growth rates of 5 to 7 percent annually are not impressive in a regional comparison and have remained at almost the

---

18 Interviews, Tehran, February 2008; see also *Financial Times,* February 11, 2008.

same level as under Khatami, who had to cope with much lower oil prices.

Iranian economists blame what they call Ahmadinejad's populist economic policy. This includes not only cash handouts to people, but also investment in service infrastructure—sports facilities, clinics, and other public buildings that local officials have asked for during the president's numerous provincial tours. Such projects, financed mainly from the Oil Stabilization Fund that Khatami had set up to prepare for future decreases in oil income, give a short boost to the construction sector but trigger inflation rather than create sustainable growth. Ahmadinejad's order to the banks to cut interest rates was propagated as an anti-inflationary measure, but effectively had the opposite effect too.[19] Inflation, which was officially at 19.2 percent per annum by 2008, realistically probably at 22 to 25 percent annually, hurt the poorest more than those who actually took bank loans to finance new real estate. Little wonder, therefore, that Ahmadinejad lost appeal among many of those who had voted for him in 2005.

International sanctions, of course, had some effect on the economic situation. This was less so for measures imposed by the Security Council in 2006 and 2007. Iranian business was particularly affected by the withdrawal, under U.S. pressure, of major international banks from the Iranian market. Major European industrial and contracting firms also reduced their business with Iran so as not to lose business in the United States or because of difficulties and delays arising from the withdrawal of banks and, especially in Germany, the reduction of export credit guarantees by the government and more cumbersome export control procedures. Much of this business was picked up by Chinese exporters and contractors or created other forms of trade diversion.[20]

---

19 Seyed Mohammad Hossein Adeli, Chairman and Chief Executive Officer, Ravand Institute for Economic and International Studies, Tehran, interview with author, February 2008.

20 In 2007, Chinese exports to Iran increased by about 62 percent while the exports from Germany to Iran decreased by 14 percent. Germany used to be one of the most important trading partners for Iran in the European Union; see Bundesagentur für Außenwirtschaft (German Office for Foreign Trade), www.bfai.de, and Statistisches Bundesamt Deutschland (Federal Statistical Office), www.destatis.de. The main trading partner of Iran remains the United Arab Emirates, with a total of bilateral trade at $11.7 billion in the Iranian year ending March 2007, with imports from the UAE forming the bulk of the exchanges at $9.2

Iranians often state, and they have a certain point, that the country has had to live with various sanctions, particularly U.S. trade and investment sanctions, for more than a quarter century, and they have become used to sanctions and to finding ways around them. Iranian businesspeople, however, became particularly nervous when Chinese banks, apparently also in response to U.S. pressure, cut down or halted their transactions with Iran.[21] Reportedly, a business delegation visited Khamene'i to complain that a further isolation of the country was not tolerable. Khamene'i will take such remonstrations seriously, even though they will likely not make him change his policies. This is particularly so as long as he fears that bowing to sanctions would only raise new demands from those who impose them—demands that might not end before some of the centerpieces of the Islamic system are dismantled.[22]

The Political Elite

The usual distinction among hard-liners, pragmatists, and reformers is useful,[23] particularly when dealing with domestic policy issues such as the economy, the limits of political participation, or cultural and moral questions. When foreign and security policies are addressed, the categories of the Islamo-nationalist right, realists, and globalizers should be added. These categories overlap with the more common ones but are not identical. Someone who is a social conservative in the cultural sphere, such as the *rahbar*, Khamene'i, and supports Ahmadinejad in his strict interpretation of Islamic mores may still be a conservative when it comes to foreign policy, but might well stand with the pragmatists or the realists in their rejection of adventurous steps.

The Iranian political landscape is not characterized by dominant parties or fixed groups but rather by factions with somewhat fluid memberships. This becomes also apparent when candidate lists are formed for elections. Despite differences among them, these factions are all acting within the constitutional framework of the Islamic Republic

---

billion; see Agence France-Presse, February 19, 2008.

21 "Chinese Banks Cut Back Business with Iran," Iran News, February 2, 2008.

22 Sadjadpour, *Reading Khamene'i*.

23 See, among many: Ray Takeyh, *Hidden Iran: Paradox and Power in the Islamic Republic* (New York: Times Books, 2006).

and are loyal to the regime even if they might want to adapt or reform it. Allowing this pluralism and choice among various factions has also given particular stability to the Islamic Republic: opposition need not be fundamental, or antiregime; it can find expression within the system. There is real competition among the various camps, voters take such competition seriously, and the electorate can remove a government or a president through peaceful means. Ray Takyeh rightly points out that none of the factions is totally out at any time: they all have a "presence" within the system.[24]

For the inner workings of the regime, it is indeed more important who is considered *khodi* or *ghayr khodi*—"one of us" or "not one of us," that is, a member of or closely related to the clerical-political networks around Khomeini and, since Khomeini's death, Khamene'i, or not—than whether someone is seen as reformist or conservative.[25] The entire elite, meanwhile, has to be concerned about its popular standing that brings a strong element of accountability into the system.

Since 2005, the Islamo-nationalist right, primarily represented by President Ahmadinejad and his friends, has had the upper edge among the factions and camps that make up the wider political elite. Western observers have generally underestimated the appeal of Ahmadinejad. The fact is, he does not appeal to *us,* the Western observers, but he does have a certain charisma. His populist attire, his easy-to-understand language, his focus on bread-and-butter issues—which actually could become politically dangerous for him if he does not deliver—have all helped to make him popular. Also, his demonstrative religiosity sets him off from both the learned clerics with their complicated theological discourses and the liberal intellectuals around former President Khatami. The cult of the hidden (twelfth) imam, to which he adheres, is looked upon with contempt by intellectuals and theologians.[26] All evidence

---

24 Ibid., 32.

25 See Johannes Reissner, *Die Rolle der Rhetorik* (Berlin: Stiftung Wissenschaft und Politik, 2000), 14.

26 According to Shiite belief, the twelfth imam (successor of the Prophet), or Mahdi, did not die but went into eternal hiding in the tenth century and will reappear at judgment day. Some of the friends of Ahmadinejad who gained political or administrative positions as part of his network share the deep conviction that the arrival of the imam is close. As M. Rida Za'iri, a midlevel cleric who was at the time also the editor in chief of the Tehran daily, *Hamshahri,* explained in a May 2006 interview with the author: "We are of the opinion that the return of the twelfth imam is

suggests that clerics, as a group, are quite unpopular. The fact that Ahmadinejad is not a cleric was certainly an advantage in the eyes of many of the people who elected him in the first place.

Generational experiences play a role, too. Ahmadinejad, himself a member of the war generation and a Revolutionary Guard instructor, has succeeded in appealing to the veterans, championing, as Ali M. Ansari puts it, "the spirit of the war . . . when faith sustained the nation and materialism was nowhere to be seen."[27] This certainly helped in setting him apart from Rafsanjani, a symbol of the founders' generation whose members have not themselves fought in the ditches. Even though some Iranian observers ask whether Ahmadinejad himself actually had much of the front-line soldier experience or was merely organizing volunteers at some distance from the war zone, he was at least able to cultivate this image.

One may, again with Ansari, also see Ahmadinejad's defiant, confrontationist attitude as a means of establishing domestic hegemony, allowing him to play the glorious leader and enabling the government to get away with more repression.[28] At least it is reasonable to assume that domestic difficulties would increase his attempts to trigger international crises or play on them. There may be more to this form of defiance, however: namely, a strong belief in what he advocates.

In that sense, Ahmadinejad's speech at the conference, "A World without Zionism," early in his presidential term may in fact express much of what he actually believes. Although he affirmatively quoted Khomeini, saying that Israel must be "wiped off the map" or, in a more correct translation, "vanish from the stage of history," Ahmadinejad did not actually advocate any action on the part of Iran to achieve this goal. Instead he expressed his belief that this would happen someday, just as the shah's regime or the regime of Saddam Hussein had fallen

---

logical." Globalization, a positive fact as such, was actually proving this, he said: "The Prophet said that when the Mahdi arrives the entire world will see and hear it. My father, thirty years ago, could not understand how something like this should be possible. But for my sons, this is no longer a puzzle: Think about September 11, or the election of the new Pope—the entire world has been able to watch what was happening, via TV, at the same time."

27 Ansari, "Iran under Ahmadinejad," 25. On the social background and ideological beliefs of Ahmadinejad, see also Olivier Roy, "Faut-il avoir peur d'Ahmadinejad?" *Politique internationale* 111 (2006): 199–208.

28 Ansari, "Iran under Ahmadinejad," 76.

in spite of all the people who said this would never happen.[29] People in his vicinity seem to have made clear to him that he had better not repeat the Khomeini quote *expressis verbis,* but even if he follows this advice, this would hardly change his beliefs about the course of history.

Confrontationalist behavior may also reflect how members of this tendency see the world. Although the United States is still the "world oppressor" or the "world of arrogance" to them,[30] followers of the Iranian neocon faction appear to be convinced that the West, particularly the United States, is declining. As one of the supporters of the president explained to this author: America is "much weaker than it appears" and "chances to survive in confronting the United States are greater than in not confronting it," and, in fact, many countries that still supported U.S. policies simply did not know how weak America was and how strong Iran was.[31] The current phase is therefore seen as a window of opportunity for Iran to pursue its interests; "resistance" to the forces of oppression or to a form of globalization in which "the West decides for the whole world"[32] is a positive force. And, of course, "we don't need anybody who tells us what we are allowed to do."[33]

Independence has an enormous value and not only for this faction, and a touch of *tiers-mondisme* is always present in this group's rhetoric. The discourse of this part of the elite is marked by what one Iranian author has called "hyper-independence," a maximalist understanding of the term that goes far beyond the common notion of national independence or sovereignty.[34] "Complete independence," as Ahmadinejad's government spokesman put it in a statement, in that sense also means that "we are not responsible for the concerns of others."[35]

---

29 For two different complete English translations of Ahmadinejad's speech, see the *New York Times,* October 30, 2005, and the Memri Special Dispatch Series, no. 1013, October 28, 2005, www.memri.org/bin/articles. cgi?Page=countries&Area=iran&ID=SP101305.

30 Ibid.

31 M. Rida Za'iri, editor in chief of *Hamshahri,* interview with author, May 2006.

32 Manoucher Mohammadi, deputy foreign minister, statement during a seminar intervention, Tehran, May 2006.

33 Za'iri, interview, May 2006.

34 Homeira Moshirzadeh, "Discursive Foundations of Iran's Nuclear Policy," *Security Dialogue* 38, no. 4 (2007): 530.

35 See "Iran Urges 'Academic Diplomacy' with West," *Tehran Times*

The realist camp, as it were, ranges from political pragmatists like Rafsanjani to conservatives or "principalists" like Larijani. They can occasionally rely on support from Khamene'i, who, on foreign and security policy issues, is seen to stand between Ahmadinejad and the realists. After all, his two representatives in the SNSC are Ali Larijani, who could be called a pragmatist principalist, and Hassan Rohani, a more classical pragmatist close to Rafsanjani. Realists advocate more engagement with the world and see that the isolation of Iran has truly negative effects on the country. They seek membership for Iran in the World Trade Organization (WTO) to attract foreign investment and to boost the Iranian economy as a whole. Realists also want to show the world that Iran is a reasonable player that accepts international law. Iran, in the words of Hassan Rohani, even wants "the non-proliferation regime to become more strengthened."[36] Moreover, realists see their country as a force that will and can help to solve crises, promote stability, and act in an overall pragmatic fashion. Support for the United States in the Kuwait war of 1991 and in the Afghanistan war of 2001 would prove the point. The United States, however, had never appreciated this support. President Bush had even responded to Iran's constructive role in Afghanistan by calling Iran a member of the "axis of evil."[37]

This realist camp is generally more tolerant with regard to people's private lives and beliefs, culturally more open in many respects. Intellectuals and cultural activists stress that Rafsanjani, during his presidential term, actually paved the way for Khatami and his explicitly reformist course. Nevertheless, some in this camp show a certain respect for Ahmadinejad, whose confrontational policies have achieved something after all: Iran is taken seriously, and it has shown the world that it can defy orders—not least so with regard to the cascades now working, against all international protests, in Natanz. In contrast with the Islamo-nationalists, the realists underline that Iran and the United States have certain common interests. They appreciate that Tehran and Washington have opened a direct channel of communication through their embassies in Baghdad. They do stress, though, that this

International, February 6, 2008.

36 Hassan Rohani, "Opening Remarks at the International Conference on Nuclear Technology and Sustainable Development," *National Interest* 2, no. 1 (2006): 7.

37 Personal communication with author, Tehran, February 2008.

was because the United States had to ask Iran for help in Iraq.[38] As to the realists, more and direct negotiations with Washington would be useful. However, the U.S. administration was seeking regime change rather than a dialogue, and it was lacking respect: "Respect is even more important than dialogue."[39]

The reformists often referred to in Iran as the friends of Khatami can hardly be described as liberals in a European sense. Their most prominent members are clerics, after all, who are firmly rooted in Islamic theology and generally committed to the religious foundations of the Islamic Republic. They certainly have a more liberal interpretation of Islam than the other factions and do not see a contradiction between Islam and democracy. Open-mindedness, domestically and internationally, became a core concept of the reformists' approach, expressed, among other ways, in Khatami's promotion of a dialogue of civilization or the establishment of an Institute for Inter-Religious Dialogue, now led by one of Khatami's closest associates. Globalization, the encounter of different cultures, and the peaceful interaction in multilateral formats are seen as positive facets of the contemporary world.

The reformist spectrum includes a number of outspoken globalists who are interested in actively bringing Iran into the world. Domestically they are the closest to what in Europe would be seen as liberal-democratic. Within this group one can find the Islamic Iran Participation Front, whose best-known leader is Reza Khatami, the brother of the former president. This faction is sometimes denounced even by parts of the reformist spectrum as too radical, which implies that they are too secular minded. Some representatives of the reformists share the nationalism of the conservatives. They also complain that Iran is inadequately treated by the great powers. Many reformists are particularly angry at the West, and at Washington especially, for undermining Khatami's presidency. While the Iranian neoconservatives would probably not have made any effort to cooperate with the United States after the terrorist attacks of September 11, 2001, and on installing a new political system in Afghanistan after the fall of the Taliban, Khatami's government did and was rewarded by being named part of the "axis

---

38 See Mahmood Vaezi and Nasser Saghafi-Ameri, "The Global Strategy of the United States in Relation with the Islamic World: A Perspective from Iran," January 2008, unpublished paper.

39 Member of SNSC, personal communication with the author, Tehran, 2006.

of evil." This, so reformists stress, only played into the hands of conservatives and hard-liners who were opposed to any cooperation with the United States. Thus, there is disappointment here with the United States for not being "sincere" and not being prepared to recognize the Iranian system.[40] Many members of the Khatami administration also complain about what they see as permanent European criticism of human rights violations.[41] Even so, reformists—like the realists—do expect initiatives from Europe and see it as a partner with whom Iran wishes to cooperate, both economically and on international issues. Domestically, the reformist camp is still in some disarray. If they ever want to return to power, they will have to learn to address social and economic issues and not only focus on the promotion of democracy and cultural dialogue.[42]

Iran's Place in the World

As the nuclear conflict has been the main issue between Iran and Europe as well as between Iran and most of the international community since 2003, it is easy to forget that there are other contentious issues, particularly regarding the Middle East. As indicated, worldviews differ among different factions in Iran, and persons and political tendencies obviously matter for chances to bring Iran's relations with its regional neighborhood and with the West in balance. There are also certain geopolitical and interest-related constants, however. Different factions within Iran may interpret them differently and draw different conclusions.

---

40 Statement made during interview with author, Tehran, May 2006. There are also observers arguing that the U.S. administration further undermined the reformists and pragmatists by calling the 2005 presidential elections in Iran illegitimate and calling upon the Iranians to boycott them. See Semiramis Akbari, *Grenzen politischer Reform- und Handlungsspielräume in Iran: die Bedeutung innenpolitischer Dynamiken für die Außenpolitik,* HSFK Report no. 9/2006 (Frankfurt a.M.: Hessische Stiftung Friedens- und Konfliktforschung [HSFK], 2006), 27. For this author, this seems a little far-fetched, as it probably overestimates the influence of the United States on Iranian voters.

41 Personal communication with author, Tehran, 2006.

42 Akbari, *Grenzen politischer Reform- und Handlungsspielräume in Iran,* 37.

A Rational Actor

It is interesting that, unlike with most other players in the international system, the "rationality question" is constantly on the table with regard to Iran and its international behavior. This is due partly to Iran being so much of a black box to many foreign observers, partly to prejudice, and not a small part to the irresponsible talk or irresponsible actions of some of Iran's leaders. Among analysts, there is quite some agreement that the Islamic Republic is indeed a rational or a "logical" actor that considers "risks and costs incurred by its actions,"[43] and whose "decisions are guided by a cost-benefit approach."[44] This implies that Iran is susceptible to incentives and disincentives from its international environment. It is clear that rationality has to be understood with regard to the aims of the regime: rational, in this sense, is what advances or protects these interests and aims at reasonable costs. And it is important not to confuse "hostility with irrationality."[45] Lack of openness, of course, as well as frequent recourse to subterfuge in discussions and negotiations make it more difficult to always understand the policy choices of a player like Iran.[46]

---

43 Ephraim Kam, *A Nuclear Iran: What Does It Mean, and What Can Be Done?* (Tel Aviv: Institute for National Security Studies, 2007), 9.

44 "Iran: Nuclear Intentions and Capabilities," 7.

45 This has been pointed out by Jon Alterman (presentation on assessing Iran's nuclear intentions and capabilities, Eighth Herzliya Conference, Herzliya, January 20–23, 2008), www.herzliyaconference.org/Eng/_Articles/Article.asp?ArticleID=2029&CategoryID=248. Alex Mintz, from the Lauder School at Herzliya, has also pointed out that, based on applied decision analysis, one can see a "strong, clear pattern of Iranian decisions being rational"; among other things, he therefore concludes that Iran would not use the bomb if it is clear that its own survival is at stake; see Alex Mintz (presentation on whether a nuclear Iran can be deterred, Eighth Herzliya Conference, Herzliya, January 20–23, 2008), www.herzliyaconference.org/Eng/_Articles/Article.asp?ArticleID=2038&CategoryID=248.

46 Diplomats in Tehran often note that their Iranian counterparts seem to have little difficulty in flatly lying to their faces. One should be cautious with any generalization about national characteristics, but different political cultures do certainly, among other things, produce different negotiating styles. One study on the Iranian way of negotiating stresses that dissimulation, disinformation, ambiguity, and manipulation are seen as acceptable by Iranian negotiators, with regard to both their own and their counterparts' behavior. See Shmuel Bar, *Iran: Cultural*

Post-Saddam Middle East

The Iraq War of 2003 can be considered a geopolitical revolution for the Middle East in more than one respect.[47] Particularly observers from the Arab world see Iran as arising from this upheaval as the main beneficiary and winner, and not a few blame the United States for this development. The picture is somewhat contradictory, however.

On the one hand, Iran's regional standing has clearly been strengthened. It gained influence as a result of the fall of Saddam Hussein, its main regional adversary for decades, as it had already gained more power from the U.S.-led overthrow of the Taliban in Afghanistan. Since the fall of the Baathist regime in Iraq, Shiite parties and individuals with very close connections to Iran play a main role there. The strongest Shiite party, the Supreme Islamic Iraqi Council (SIIC; previously called SCIRI, the Supreme Council for the Islamic Revolution in Iraq), was founded as a resistance movement against the Saddam regime in Iran and with Iranian support. Its militia, formerly the Badr Corps, now the Badr organization, whose members have been recruited in large numbers into the new Iraqi security forces, is Iranian trained. Many of the leading Shiite but also a number of Kurdish politicians have spent years in Iranian exile. The more radical movement of Moktada al-Sadr has also sought and received Iranian support, mainly from the Iranian Revolutionary Guard Corps (Pasdaran).

These connections, the transnational confessional link to the Shiite majority population in Iraq, and, of course, geographic proximity have certainly made Iran the most influential foreign actor in Iraq after—or politically even on a par with—the United States.[48] In March 2008, Ahmadinejad became the first Iranian president to visit Iraq. This was seen as a sign of support for the Iraqi government but also as a demonstration of influence in a country still controlled by U.S. forces.

Iran's geopolitical reach into the Levant was demonstrated, though not for the first time, during the summer war of 2006 between Israel and Lebanon's Hezbollah, which was openly supported by Iran. Iran's position in Lebanon had already been enhanced by the withdrawal of

---

Values, Self-Images and Negotiating Behavior, Herzliya Paper (Herzliya: Interdisciplinary Center, October 2004).

47 See Volker Perthes, *Bewegung im Mittleren Osten: Internationale Geopolitik und regionale Dynamiken nach dem Irak-Krieg,* SWP-Studie 32/2004 (Berlin: Stiftung Wissenschaft und Politik, September 2004).

48 Ansari, "Iran under Ahmadinejad," 2007.

the Israeli army in 2000 and, probably more so, by that of the Syrian army in 2005,[49] which reduced Syria's influence over and ability to physically constrain Hezbollah.[50] Ahmadinejad and, even more so, Hezbollah were able to gain popularity in countries like Egypt during and immediately after the 2006 war. Iran's political influence is not appreciated but is considered a fact by the Arab states. Saudi Arabia, which is regarded as the main patron of Lebanon's Sunni community, has therefore accepted Iran as an interlocutor in its efforts to find a solution to Lebanon's domestic political crisis. The popularity of the Iranian president and of Hezbollah in other Arab countries has again waned, nonetheless, since sectarian undertones became louder in the regional political discourse.

Iran's influence in the Palestinian territories has remained limited despite Tehran's overt support for the Palestinian "resistance." Seen from Iran, the victory of Hamas in the legislative elections of 2006 was a good thing. It proved to Iran's political elite that people in the Middle East, if given the choice, would vote for Islamists. The international boycott of the Hamas-led government also offered Iran an opportunity to make a quasi-official entry into Palestine and respond to pledges for material support, not only from political groups like Hamas and the Palestinian Islamic Jihad, but also from the Palestinian Authority. One can safely assume that Iran has continued to support Hamas authorities in the Gaza Strip after the 2007 split in the Authority.

There are other indicators for Iran's new, strong status in the region. Iran's President Ahmadinejad was admitted, if more or less at his own invitation, as a guest at the 2007 summit meeting of the Gulf Cooperation Council (GCC) in Qatar, the regional grouping made up of the monarchies on the Arabian peninsula. Efforts are under way to reestablish relations with Egypt. This may be as much an Egyptian as an Iranian interest, but it is not necessarily what Washington would ask the Egyptian government to do.

The United States itself had to recognize the importance of Iran, not least for developments in Iraq. As a result, and in spite of continued tensions and Washington's rather concrete accusations that Iran

---

49 David Menashri, "After the War: Iranian Power and its Limitations," in *The Second Lebanon War: Strategic Perspectives,* ed. Shlomo Brom and Meir Elran (Tel Aviv: Institute for National Security Studies, 2007), 155.

50 Volker Perthes, "The Syrian Solution," *Foreign Affairs* 85, no. 6 (2006): 33–40.

continued to offer material, lethal support to Iraqi militants, the two sides have met in the multilateral context of the so-called Iraq Neighbors conferences (which bring together Iraq, its direct neighbors, Egypt, Bahrain, the permanent members of the Security Council, and the Group of Eight) and also began direct talks on the ambassadorial level in Baghdad in May 2007.

The EU had less difficulty accepting Iran as an important political player. Javier Solana, the EU high representative for the Common Foreign and Security Policy, even spoke of Iran as a "rising power" and a "key country in the Middle East" in his statement to the European Parliament. He indicated, certainly to enhance the success of his diplomatic dealings with Tehran, that this development was appreciated in Europe.[51]

On the other hand, Iran also has good reasons to feel strategically more uncomfortable given that it is virtually surrounded by the United States. Put yourself in the shoes, say, of a member of Iran's National Security Council and look at a map of Iran's surroundings, and you cannot avoid seeing that U.S. combat troops are stationed in Iraq and Afghanistan, the U.S. fleet is plowing the waters of the Gulf, Turkey is a NATO member, Washington has declared Pakistan a major non-NATO ally, and even Azerbaijan is engaged in military cooperation with the United States.[52]

The Arab states, despite their recognition of the importance of dealing with Iran, are wary of Iran's "rise": they fear, rightly or wrongly, Shiite influence among their own population. The concept of a "Shiite axis" reaching from Iran, through Iraq and Syria, to Lebanon has been traded mainly by the Sunni elites in GCC countries and Jordan and has fostered a confessionalization of regional discourses. The Arab states have made efforts, unsuccessful so far, to drive a wedge between Damascus and Tehran, not least so by encouraging Israel to resume peace talks with Syria. Voices from the Arab Gulf countries that call Iran a danger and ask the United States and the international community to contain Iran have become louder, and not only with regard to Iran's nuclear program. Washington has openly attempted to rally the Arab

---

51 "Statement to the European Parliament on Iran by Javier Solana," Brussels, January 30, 2008, SO36/08, www.consilium.europa.eu/ueDocs/cms_Data/docs/pressData/en/discours/98535.pdf.

52 Robert McMahon, "Azerbaijani President Stresses Military Cooperation with U.S. in Afghanistan, Iraq—but Not Iran," *News Briefing,* Council on Foreign Relations, New York, April 26, 2006.

states against Iran while trying to promote the idea of an (anti-Iranian) alliance of "moderate" Arab states and Israel[53] and is increasing arms sales to its Arab allies.[54] Arab leaders have no interest, though, in openly allying themselves with the United States against a neighbor.

From an Iranian perspective, Washington is not only making an effort to weaken Iran's regional reach, but also attempts to undermine its regime. International pressure on Iran has definitely mounted since the dispute over Tehran's nuclear program was transferred from the IAEA to the UN Security Council and a first Security Council resolution (1696) on that matter was passed in the shadow of the Lebanon war in July 2006. So it does not come as a surprise that Iran vacillates among feelings of strength, wariness, and insecurity.

Domestic Debates, Fears, and Interests

Trying to analyze the Iranian elite's perception of their country's relations with the rest of the world, one is tempted to simply distinguish two tendencies: one that displays little trust, particularly in the West and the West's intentions toward Iran, and another that displays no trust at all. It is clear that those whom we have labeled the Islamo-nationalist right have the least trust of all.

Their conviction, however, that Iran has always been targeted, been an object of other powers' maneuverings, and been treated wrongly over the centuries is widely shared by other members of the elite and, as far as this can be gauged, by a major part of the general population. In contrast with the Islamo-nationalists, realists and reformists tend to distinguish among the United States, Europe, and others and mix their skepticism about the intentions of foreign powers with somewhat cautious optimism. To cite Hassan Rohani: the Iranian people, he says, "have concluded that the West . . . is in permanent conflict with our independence, national sovereignty, development and progress." However, "we feel that Europe, in principle, is not seeking to deprive Iran of its legitimate interests."[55]

---

53 George W. Bush, "President Bush Discusses Importance of Freedom in the Middle East" (speech in Abu Dhabi, United Arab Emirates, January 13, 2008), www.whitehouse.gov/news/releases/2008/01/20080113-1.html.

54 Robin Wright, "U.S. Plans New Arms Sales to Gulf Allies. $20 Billion Deal Includes Weapons For Saudi Arabia," *Washington Post,* July 28, 2007.

55 Rohani, "Opening Remarks."

There is, of course, a historical basis for this mistrust and skepticism. After all, Iran has been invaded or under semicolonial control by, among others, the Arabs, the Mongols, Britain, and Russia. The United States helped to overthrow a popular prime minister and reinstall the shah in 1953, and most of the Arab states as well as the United States and other Western countries supported Iraq in the eight-year Iraq-Iran war. The feeling of constant victimization may be seen as a facet of Iran's political culture. It can also easily turn into an ideology. It certainly helps to strengthen the belief that Iran has to defend its independence at all costs, that it must not bow to the will of foreigners, or that it has to resist the oppressive forces in the world.[56] Self-sufficiency and self-reliance are often quoted as principles of Iran's national policy. But the Iranian elite is not isolationist and would not question the need for Iran to engage with the world. Anything else would, in fact, be deeply irrational for a country with Iran's geography, history, and resource endowment. Isolation is seen as something that is imposed from abroad.

There are different views within the regime elite about the principles that should guide international relations. Somewhat simplified, one could say that while the entire elite stresses independence, Iran's realists emphasize international legality, and globalists add to that the principle of intercultural dialogue. Islamo-nationalists, in their own words, would hold that the "only organizing principle" to address the world's problems is "the principle of justice among nations and states."[57] Justice, of course, can be a rather transcendent concept and is not necessarily the same as international law.

All over the elite spectrum there is a strong feeling that Iran is a rising power and has to be treated as such. Two leading realists state that the "new regional environment after the demise of the Baathist regime of Saddam in Iraq and the Taliban regime in Afghanistan has boosted Iran's influence and its soft power projection." They also refer to what they see as "the Shias' geopolitical advantages and the fact that

---

56 See Homeira Moshirzadeh, "Discursive Foundations of Iran's Nuclear Policy," *Security Dialogue* 38, no. 4 (2007): 528. Moshirzadeh explains how the "meta-discourses" of independence, of justice, and, at times, of resistance (help to) give meaning to Iran's foreign policies (and its nuclear policy in particular).

57 Manouchehr Mohammadi, "Principles of Iran's Foreign Policy," *Iranian Journal of International Affairs* 19, no. 1 (2007): 5. Mohammadi, a deputy foreign minister seen as particularly close to Ahmadinejad, explicitly refers to the Iranian president's thinking in this passage.

all major oil and gas fields in the Persian Gulf region are located in the Shia-dominated regions."[58] The new situation is seen as an opportunity. After all, as one influential interlocutor has stated: "Our friends are now ruling in Iraq and in Afghanistan."[59] But it is also seen as a threat.

Reformists and pragmatists clearly define Iran's foreign policy in terms of national interest, they play down ideological overtones to almost zero, and they make clear that even though they are not always happy with the status quo, it is not upon Iran to change it. The power that actively changed the regional status quo, after all, was the United States, which, since 2003, had to be accepted as a new neighbor. Relations with the United States are in every respect, even in their absence, the most important issue, especially when it comes to security questions. Individual European states, particularly Germany and Italy, may enjoy more trust, or rather less distrust. The EU is Iran's main bilateral trading partner.[60]

However, as one Iranian diplomat once in charge of EU-relations explained: the EU is "difficult to work with. It is difficult to understand whether you have to lobby the commission, the presidency, or the individual countries." The EU, he continued, also had not been very supportive to Iran, even under Khatami, whom Europeans misconstrued as a Gorbachev who would eventually dismantle the system and thereby weakened him.[61] Certainly, neither the EU nor any European state can match the interest that the United States and its policies draw in policy discussions or in the public debate. The general feeling among Iranians, not only the elite, is that Iran should deal with Washington on equal footing, which is only consequent if one perceives, as realists explicitly do, the relationship between the United States in terms of "rivalry" or "geopolitical competition."[62]

Complaints are constant that the United States does not respect Iran and its system. In the words of Amir Mohebian, a conservative thinker and author: "The United States, up till now, does not accept our reality.

---

58 See Vaezi and Saghafi-Ameri, "Global Strategy of the United States in Relation with the Islamic World: A Perspective from Iran."

59 Personal communication with author, Tehran, February 2008.

60 In 2006, the EU provided 33.4 percent of Iran's total imports; in 2007 this dropped to less than 28 percent. Iran enjoys a trade surplus with the EU.

61 Iranian diplomat, personal communications with the author, 2004, 2006.

62 For example, Vaezi and Saghafi-Ameri, "The Global Strategy of the United States in Relation with the Islamic World: A Perspective from Iran."

They think the Islamic revolution was only an accident."[63] Particularly on the conservative side, there are strong fears that Washington is trying to trigger a "velvet revolution" in Iran through Iranian civil society activists. Parts of the elite also fear that the United States is instigating ethnic unrest in Iran, a fear that is supported by the fact that at least some U.S. commentators have advocated exactly such a policy.[64]

Realists and reformists have for some time openly expressed their intent to reestablish relations with the United States, and even conservatives and Islamo-nationalists have come to accept the idea that U.S.-Iran relations could improve. This has become much easier since Ayatollah Khamene'i publicly stated: "Undoubtedly, the day the relations with America prove beneficial for the Iranian nation, I will be the first to approve of that."[65] With this somewhat astonishing remark, Khamene'i opened the floor for public debate about the way in which relations with the United States could be resumed. After all, this was now being defined as a matter of proper timing. And even though he added that this time had not yet come, he also signaled to his domestic audience as well as to Washington that he was the person in charge who eventually would take such an important decision.

There is general consensus in Tehran that no president would be able to open high-level talks with the United States, let alone reestablish diplomatic relations, without the explicit backing of Khamene'i. Even the limited ambassadorial-level talks between the United States and Iran in Baghdad had, in fact, been publicly sanctioned by the leader some time before they came about, against the opinion of Ahmadinejad, as insiders confided at that time. By 2008, most Iranian observers also agreed that Ahmadinejad, given Khamene'i's blessing, would be willing to take the initiative for a rapprochement with Washington and that he or another conservative would have more chance of doing this than a reformist who would meet more ideological opposition from the right.

---

63 Amir Mohebian, interview with author, Tehran, February 2008. Mohebian is editor of the conservative newspaper *Risalat.*

64 See Roger Cohen, "Time to Call in the Iranian Chips," *International Herald Tribune,* July 5, 2007.

65 "No Benefit in U.S. Ties for Now," Office of the Supreme Leader Sayyid Ali Khamene'i, January 3, 2008, www.leader.ir/langs/en/index. php?p=contentShow&id=3661.

It was also assumed that Ahmadinejad would have a personal interest in such a development. Bringing back U.S.-Iranian relations would earn him enormous popularity and could, if it were to happen early enough, be the safest way to win a second presidential term. There seem to be some illusions in policy-advising circles in Tehran about the extent to which President Bush or his successor would be prepared to accept President Ahmadinejad as a partner. Not only is he not the prime decision maker, he has also burned many bridges with his Holocaust denial and offensive statements with regard to Israel. Thus, he has made it extremely difficult for any Western leader to sit down with him for a friendly encounter. Many Iranian policy pundits reject this argument and point, astonishingly perhaps, to the pragmatism of the United States, which eventually supersedes such personal or ideological considerations. One should remember, as one observer put it, the visit to Iran of former U.S. national security adviser Robert McFarlane, who carried with him a planeload of arms in the midst of the Iraq-Iran War. In the West, the episode is usually referred to as the Iran-Contra affair.

It would not be the first time for a postwar Iranian government to seek a rapprochement with Washington. There is little disagreement that the government of Mohammad Khatami played a constructive role in the international efforts to oust the Taliban and establish a new order in Afghanistan, particularly at the Petersburg Conference in November 2001.[66] In 2003, shortly after the U.S. invasion of Iraq, the Khatami government tried to explore the conditions for a grand bargain between the two states. It even sent a rather concrete proposal to the United States. In this "road map," as it was called, Iran offered to drop its material support for Palestinian militants; support the transformation of Hezbollah into a purely political organization; accept a two-state solution between Israel and Palestine; and become transparent on its nuclear program in exchange for mutual respect, the abolition of U.S. sanctions, access to nuclear energy, some form of security arrangements, and a revocation of Iran's placement on the "axis of evil." The U.S. administration rejected the proposal.[67]

66 See James Dobbins, "How to Talk to Iran," *Washington Post,* July 22, 2007.

67 See Hillary Mann, "U.S. Diplomacy with Iran: The Limits of Tactical Engagement" (statement to the Subcommittee on National Security and Foreign Affairs, Committee on Government Oversight and Reform, U.S. House of Representatives, November 7, 2007); Glenn Kessler, "2003

Iraq, Afghanistan, Israel

U.S.-Iran relations are largely determined by Iran's policies toward Iraq, toward Israel and the Arab-Israeli conflict and peace process, and toward Afghanistan. Of course, the strained relationship with Washington and the U.S. presence in Iraq and Afghanistan also affect Iran's policies to these two countries to some extent, which sometimes leads to contradictions in Iranian behavior.

It has been expedient for both the United States and Iran to focus on Iraq since limited official U.S.-Iranian talks were resumed in 2007. This is a place where interests of both states clash and also overlap. Both Iran and the United States have supported the democratically elected Iraqi government, and both have an interest in the stabilization of Iraq. Iran is torn between its appreciation that the United States overthrew Iran's worst and strongest enemy, the regime of Saddam Hussein, and its apprehension with regard to the massive U.S. troop presence in its immediate neighborhood. Iran therefore demands the withdrawal of the "occupying forces from Iraq," but, notably, "at the earliest possible time,"[68] not an immediate withdrawal.

Iran is interested in a stable neighborhood and in a stable Iraq, and it expresses this interest explicitly. What is not said so clearly is that Iran, as one veteran diplomat in Tehran put it, wants Iraq to be stable but not to be strong.[69] Iran has not forgotten the eight years of war with Iraq. From an Iranian perspective, the return of a strong, centralized regime in Baghdad is a nightmare, even more so if that regime was armed by and allied with the United States. Iran, therefore, prefers a federal system in Iraq. Iranian policy experts have also underlined the importance of Iran reaching out to all communities, thus relying not only on the Shiite majority in Iraq, and fostering regional cooperation among Iran, Iraq, and Syria.[70]

Memo Says Iranian Leader Backed Talks," *Washington Post,* February 14, 2007; Nicholas D. Kristof, "Diplomacy at Its Worst," *New York Times,* April 29, 2007.

68 Mohammadi, "Principles of Iran's Foreign Policy," 8.

69 Iranian diplomat, personal communication with author, Tehran, February 2008.

70 "New Equations in Iraq: Positions Taken by Iran, the United States & Arab Countries," CSR Papers no. 1 (Tehran: Center for Strategic Research, undated [2006?]), 24–29.

Iran also certainly does not want Iraq to become a satellite of the United States. As long as U.S. forces remain in Iraq, Iran wants them to be occupied rather than being able to use Iraq as a base for the containment of or possible military action against Iran. This gives a certain short-term rationale for the support of Iraqi militants, such as the Mahdi Army of Moktada al-Sadr, who can keep some heat on the U.S. troops even if that undermines the stability of Iraq and makes life more difficult for the Iranian-supported government. Obviously, different policy goals are at cross-purposes here, and different actors, such as the Revolutionary Guards and the SNSC, may have different priorities. One need not assume that Iran has a thought-through strategy for Iraq. Experience from the United States or Europe tells us that strategies are often lacking even where policymakers see vital interests at stake. It is quite reasonable to assume, however, that the pendulum would swing toward the interest in stabilizing Iraq rather than supporting militants if Iran were assured that Washington was seeking neither a permanent military presence in Iraq nor regime change in Iran.[71]

Similar considerations play a role with regard to Afghanistan. Iran has been generally supportive of the new regime in Kabul but also interested in maintaining influence, particularly in western border regions. U.S. officials have repeatedly accused Iran of extending some support to militant oppositional forces in Afghanistan. Although Iran denies this charge, parts of the regime are likely to use such instruments, again not so much to actually undermine the Karzai government but to signal to Washington that Iran has means to hurt U.S. interests. Iran has definitely no interest in the return to power of the Taliban, and it is not outright opposed to the presence of NATO and other foreign forces in Afghanistan, but it blames NATO and the Western powers engaged in Afghanistan for the instability and lack of progress in that country. The drug trade from Afghanistan is causing real problems for Iran, and the Iranian government has shown an interest in cooperating with foreign drug enforcement agencies and receiving support from Europe to better control the border regions.

Another challenge for Iran is the huge number of refugees and irregular migrants from Afghanistan. Given high unemployment in

---

71 It is noteworthy that, according to U.S. officials, Iraqi militants, notably the Mahdi Army of Moktada al-Sadr, decreased at least for some time after the beginning of the formal trilateral talks among Iran, the United States, and Iraq in Baghdad. See Karen DeYoung, "Iran Cited in Iraq's Decline in Violence," *Washington Post,* December 23, 2007.

Iran, the presence of so many Afghans who usually work for lowest wages causes domestic frictions. The Iranian government has therefore made efforts to distinguish between refugees and irregular economic migrants, and in 2007 Iran began to repatriate many of the latter. This caused some friction with the Afghan government. Aside from the practical difficulties involved in dealing with the refugees, Iranians see this as another case, and here they have a point, where the international community simply fails to acknowledge Tehran's constructive role.[72]

Closely connected to the situation in Afghanistan, Iran is also increasingly concerned with regard to Pakistan. Even in the past, the Iranian elite felt somewhat uneasy about a major Sunni power with a nuclear bomb at its borders—nothing, however, that prevented that same elite to do business with A. Q. Khan's nuclear supermarket. Meanwhile, there are deeper fears that parts of Pakistan could come under the control of another version of the Taliban and the entire country may be destabilized. Again the West, particularly the United States, is blamed for this development. Not only were Western states backing the wrong people in Pakistan and thereby encouraging them to pursue their dangerous policies, the West, so the argument goes, was also irrational in focusing so much on Iran's (peaceful) nuclear program while it ignored the risks emanating from Pakistan.

The most contentious issue in Iran's relations with the West is Israel. Enmity toward Israel has become part of the ideology of the state or of the revolutionary identity of the Islamic Republic. Were Iran to make peace with Israel, little of the revolution, at least of its international dimension, would be left. Evidently, parts of the Iranian elite would like to reach that stage.

For the conservative core, however, Israel remains not only a useful external enemy. Many here are deeply convinced that Israel should not be there; that it is illegitimate, a colonial implantation; that its very existence is an assault on Islam and, of course, a historical injustice done to the Palestinian people—a conviction that is widely shared in much of the wider Muslim world. It is notable that Iran's position with regard to Israel is rarely presented in religious terms but in the secular terms of regional politics, oppression, and resistance. As one of the

---

72 According to the Office of the United Nations High Commissioner for Refugees, Iran does a remarkable job in dealing with refugees on its territory. They receive free medical health care and primary education. Iran does not get any funding for its refugee camps or its health and education programs from the international community.

representatives of Ahmadinejad's Islamo-nationalist faction puts it: the Islamic Republic "believes that the root cause of the current crisis in the Middle East is Israel and its aggressive behavior." Israel, continues the author, who also seeks to defend the Iranian leadership against accusations of anti-Semitism, is built on "a racist political ideology that is the root cause of instability in the region and has no relation with the nature and logic of a great divine religion as Judaism."[73]

For Israel and the international community the question is not so much what the ruling circles in Iran think about Israel, but what they do in reality. The Iranian government has rejected the efforts of the United States and the so-called Middle East Quartet to restart the Israeli-Palestinian peace process, and it rejects a two-state solution. It gives substantial material support and training not only to its Lebanese ally, Hezbollah, but also to Hamas and the Palestinian Islamic Jihad, celebrating their "resistance" against the "Zionist entity" and encouraging them to continue the armed struggle. And, of course, Israelis cannot but be concerned about the nuclear program, not only, but particularly, since Mahmoud Ahmadinejad became president. Little wonder therefore that Israel seriously discusses all options, including prominently an Israeli military attack against Iran's nuclear installations.[74] Interestingly, the Iranian elite does not seem to consider this a real option. Possible U.S. military action is a matter of concern. But the threat perception with regard to Israel is low, which also may reflect the realization that Israel will not initiate hostilities against the Islamic Republic unless it really feels threatened. On its part, Iran has always avoided getting involved in a direct military confrontation with Israel. Nothing indicates that even the hard-liners around Ahmadinejad would want to change this. A government under a more pragmatic leadership would certainly change the tone and rhetoric and simply shift the policy focus to more relevant issues, notably Iran's relationship with the West.

Iran's realists argue that the president's aggressive statements about Israel are detrimental to Iran's interests and stand in the way of better U.S.-Iran relations.[75] Foreign policy, Hassan Rohani explained in a

---

73 Mohammadi, "Principles of Iran's Foreign Policy," 9.

74 See most comprehensively, Kam, *A Nuclear Iran,* 32–41; also see Reuven Pedatzur, "The Iranian Nuclear Threat and the Israeli Options," *Contemporary Security Policy* 28, no. 3 (2007): 513–541.

75 See Vaezi and Saghafi-Ameri, "The Global Strategy of the United States in Relation with the Islamic World: A Perspective from Iran," p. 11.

lecture in Tehran, was about choosing the right instruments to reduce threats and guarantee the country's interests, not about "bragging and using improper language."[76] While certainly no friends of Israel, they are in no way "religious" about it. Rather, in their view, Iran should realize that Western commitments to Israel's security are serious and consider them "as a reality in any foreign policy calculations."[77] This would match the approach of reformist politicians like Khatami who, while never calling for a recognition, let alone peace with Israel, has occasionally stated that Iran would eventually "not be more Palestinian than the Palestinians" and accept any solution the Palestinian people were prepared to accept.

Wider Environment

Most Arab states actively supported Saddam Hussein in his war against Iran. Successive Iranian governments have made efforts to repair relations with the monarchies in the Arabian peninsula and other major Arab states such as Egypt. Mutual mistrust and policy controversies make this a very slow process. Relations with the United Arab Emirates, particularly with Dubai, are exceptional. The UAE is by far Iran's most important trading partner, there is a substantial Iranian minority living and making business in Dubai, and the rulers of the emirate are the main proponents of what could be called conflict reduction through trade.

As regards Saudi Arabia and the other Gulf monarchies, confessional tensions and the discrimination that Shiites have been suffering in some of these Arab Gulf states have strained relations, as do the strong defense and security ties these countries maintain with the United States. Most of the Arab states are rather wary with regard to Iran, its regional ambitions, and not least its nuclear program. At the same time, there is no interest on the part of most Arab states in a military confrontation between the United States and Iran that could easily destabilize the entire Persian Gulf area. Gulf Arab states have made

---

Ahmadinejad's statements, they argue, have become "one of the most important pretexts" for those in the United States who "try to give a negative image" of Iran.

76 Quoted from *al-Hayat*, February 29, 2008.

77 Nasser Saghafi-Ameri, "The Strategic Interaction between Iran and Europe," (Tehran: Center for Strategic Research, Department of Foreign Policy Research, May 2006), 20.

their own efforts to reach out to Ahmadinejad, and they are not enthusiastic about U.S. appeals to confront Iran together. At the same time, they expect that the West and the international community somehow take care of the Iranian nuclear threat. Saudi Arabia and its partners express their uneasiness with Iran's nuclear ambitions by, among other things, announcing their own nuclear programs and, at the same time, proposing the establishment of a nuclear arms–free zone in the Persian Gulf and a common enrichment center in a third country.

Two states are of particular interest for Iran: Lebanon, given more long-standing transnational links between the Shiite communities and clergy; and Syria, the only state that stood with Iran during the Iraq-Iran War. The Iranian-Syrian relationship is probably the only bilateral relationship of Iran that could be called strategic. This partnership has allowed policy coordination and mutual support in crises, even in situations where policy differences were apparent. Thus, Iran's only mild criticism of Syrian efforts to resume the peace process showed that both states are prepared to accept the national interest of the other. In contrast with a simplified image of power politics and coalitions in the Middle East, the interests of the two states are not identical, even where they overlap. Thus, both Damascus and Tehran support Hezbollah, the main Shiite party and militia in Lebanon. Damascus, however, sees Hezbollah as a tool that it is prepared to use to put pressure on Israel or the Lebanese government or to prevent an unfriendly government in Lebanon establishing its authority, even at the expense of the standing or popularity of Hezbollah. Tehran, in contrast, has an interest in Hezbollah's survival and in helping it acquire a greater stake in Lebanon's political setup.

The protection of national interest is largely the principle that in Iran's view should dominate bilateral relations. This is also evident with respect to Iran's relations to Turkey. Despite Turkey's NATO membership, Iran entertains solid relations with Turkey, which has even become a major trade and investment partner. Similarly, Iran has a strong interest in relations with India. Even though there are occasional critical statements with regard to India's defense cooperation with Israel, Iran sees India as a strategic partner, not least with regard to the so-called IPI (Iran-Pakistan-India) as "peace pipeline." The reluctant partner here is India, not least so because it has to take U.S. opposition to the project into consideration. Relations also soured for a while when India, against the warnings of Tehran, supported the

IAEA decision to refer the conflict over Iran's nuclear program to the United Nations Security Council.

With Russia the story is more complex. There remains the historical burden of Russia and the Soviet Union having occupied parts of Iran. The Soviet Union became an important source for arms deliveries in the Iraq-Iran war, and Russian companies have maintained that position. On its part, Iran has pursued a clear national interest policy vis-à-vis the Soviet Union and Russia. Iran refrained, for example, from any incitement of Muslims in Russia or support for Chechen rebels. Today, both countries have an interest in counterbalancing U.S. influence in the Middle East. Russia has completed the Bushehr nuclear power station, and Russia and Iran are major trade partners. They remain skeptical partners, though. Russian policymakers do not trust the purported solely nonmilitary purpose of Iran's nuclear program, and Iran has doubts about Russia's reliability as a source of fuel for Bushehr. There is also some apprehension in Iran with regard to Russian intentions to monopolize energy flows from the Caspian region to Europe through its territory. Iran and Russia, here, are clearly rivals. From an Iranian perspective, the relationship with Russia is useful and important, but it is a "tactical alliance," rather than a strategic relationship.[78]

China is increasingly seen by Iran as a partner for economic interactions where European companies are not available. Ahmadinejad has been promoting a Look East policy, which is indeed more promising than his parallel attempts to form an alliance with other more politically isolated leaders such as Hugo Chavez of Venezuela. In 2008, following an initial agreement between France and the United Arab Emirates about the establishment of a French military base in Abu Dhabi, there was some talk in Iran that the Islamic Republic could consider offering a naval base to China in the Persian Gulf. Most likely there would be little interest in Beijing for such an option, and ideas of that kind were meant to serve as a warning to the United States and France that Western powers might not be the only ones militarizing the Gulf.

China, as noted, has played a major role in substituting goods and services that Western firms were no longer prepared to deliver under official and unofficial sanctions. Iran was therefore particularly

---

78 See the very useful paper by Ghoncheh Tazmini, "Russian and Iranian Relations in Perspective," *Ravand Policy Paper* no. 1 (Tehran: Ravand Institute for Economic and International Studies, 2008), 19.

concerned when not only Russia, but also China, supported Western efforts to put pressure on Iran over its nuclear program.

Iran's Nuclear Program:
A Story of Winning Time and Losing Opportunities

"The Security Council passes more and more resolutions; Iran installs more and more centrifuges."[79] Iran's nuclear story did not begin with the Islamic Republic. A nuclear program was first established in the 1970s under the shah and with Western support, and, while ostensibly for civilian purposes only, there was little doubt that it was indeed designed to give the regime the ability to produce a nuclear weapon in a rather short time should the regional situation demand it.[80] The program was discontinued after the revolution. Khomeini was skeptical of the technology and of the dependence on the West that the program implied as well as ethically opposed to the idea of weapons of mass destruction.[81] The West, on its part, had little confidence in the new regime. The German company Siemens eventually withdrew from the Bushehr nuclear power station project that it had begun. Iran failed to meet its financial obligations as a partner in the French-led uranium enrichment consortium, Eurodif, and was eventually pushed out of the company when, in the early 1990s, Iran asked for a delivery of enriched uranium.[82]

Iran's own nuclear program was restarted in the second half of the 1980s. The bitter experience of being attacked with chemical weapons in the war with Iraq had reportedly made the Iranian leadership decide to resume a program with both civilian and military purposes. The official part of the nuclear program included the resumption of work

---

79 Gholamali Khoshrou, former deputy foreign minister of Iran (comments on the development of the nuclear issue between Iran and the international community, Stiftung Wissenschaft und Politik, Berlin, May 2007).

80 See Colin Dueck and Ray Takeyh, "Iran's Nuclear Challenge," *Political Science Quarterly* 122, no. 2 (2007): 189–190.

81 See Shmuel Bar, Rachel Machtiger, and Shmuel Bachar, "Iranian Nuclear Decision Making under Ahmadinejad" (draft, Herzliya, 2008), 11–13.

82 For details, see Oliver Meier, "Iran and Foreign Enrichment: A Troubled Model," *Arms Control Today,* January/February 2006, www.armscontrol.org/act/2006_01-02/JANFEB-iranenrich.asp.

at the Bushehr nuclear power plant. In 1990, the Soviet Union agreed to finish the reactor and to cooperate with Iran on nuclear research for peaceful purposes. Another part of the program consisted of hidden activities to procure centrifuges and other technology that would allow Iran to eventually master the nuclear fuel cycle. As a member of the NPT, Iran should have reported these activities, which were not illegal as such, to the IAEA, but it failed to do so, thereby breaching its NPT obligations. Internationally, there is little doubt today that Iran also pursued, as an NPT member, an illegal weaponization program that most probably included studies on explosives and the design of a nuclear warhead.[83]

In the summer of 2002, while the preparations for the U.S. invasion of Iraq were under way, Iran's hidden program, including the enrichment facility at Natanz and a planned heavy-water nuclear reactor in Arak, became publicly known from intelligence provided by an Iranian opposition group, the Mujahideen-e Khalq. While not directly related, this disclosure and the overthrow of the regime of Saddam Hussein by force of U.S. arms in the spring of 2003 marked the beginning of the yet unfinished story of international diplomatic activities with regard to the Iranian nuclear program. The Iranian elite had to assess the new regional situation with its opportunities and threats—the fall of its archenemy in Iraq, the presence of U.S. forces on its doorsteps, and a U.S. administration apparently intent on forcing regime change not only in Baghdad.

As outlined further above, Iran's reaction included an offer to the United States of negotiations on all contentious issues—the nuclear program, terrorism, Iranian support for Hezbollah and Hamas—and its preparedness to open up its program and cooperate more to the letter with the IAEA. It is also logical that the Iranian elite, as assumed by the 2007 U.S. NIE on Iran, at that point or somewhat later decided to discontinue the weaponization part of the nuclear program. The Iraqi threat was gone. U.S. power projection into the region was overwhelming. A crash program to achieve nuclear deterrence against the United States

---

83 "Iran: Nuclear Intentions and Capabilities"; "Implementation of the NPT Safeguards Agreement and Relevant Provisions of Security Council Resolutions 1737 (2006) and 1747 (2007) in the Islamic Republic of Iran, Report by the Director General," GOV/2008/4, February 22, 2008, www.iaea.org/Publications/Documents/Board/2008/gov2008-4. pdf; see also: Thérèse Delpech, "Iran: UN Rapport Explosif," *Politique internationale* 118 (Winter 2007–2008), 143–151.

may have been impossible and would have needed high-level political decisions that probably neither Khamene'i nor president Khatami favored, and the decision to open up the program for inspections had been taken. And while Washington was not prepared to respond positively to the Iranian initiative for a rapprochement, at least the Europeans were prepared to talk and offer a perspective for a better relationship between the Islamic Republic and the West.

Iranian Nuclear File between the EU-3 and the Security Council
Remarkably, in the Iranian nuclear case, Europe adopted a proactive approach rather than limiting itself to supporting or criticizing U.S. policies. Washington initially accepted letting the Europeans go ahead. It remained skeptical about the European way, however, and only belatedly, arguably too late, decided to support the EU initiative publicly in the spring of 2005.

France, Germany, and the United Kingdom, now generally referred to as the EU-3, in close coordination with Javier Solana, the EU's high representative of the Common Foreign and Security Policy, started direct negotiations over a nuclear deal with Tehran in summer 2003. The Europeans acknowledged Iran's right, as a sovereign state and a signatory of the NPT, to operate a peaceful nuclear program. Given almost two decades of concealed nuclear activities by the Iranian government, however, they made it clear that without a voluntary decision to cease or at least suspend enrichment temporarily, they would not and could not trust Iran's repeatedly stated intentions to use its nuclear program for civilian purposes only.

In October 2003, following negotiations with the EU-3, Iran agreed to sign the Additional Protocol with wider IAEA inspection rights than those every NPT member has to agree to and to suspend enrichment and reprocessing activities. In November 2004, after further talks, Iran and the three EU countries concluded the so-called Paris agreement in which Iran reaffirmed its decision to voluntarily suspend enrichment activities as long as serious negotiations were being conducted. Over the following months, the Europeans insisted on a cessation of Iran's enrichment program, and Iranian negotiators maintained their position that Iran would never permanently give up enrichment but was prepared to seek an agreement on "objective guarantees" that would ensure the peaceful use of all nuclear activities. In August 2005, the EU-3 presented a draft "Framework for a Long-Term Agreement." It mainly offered access to the international nuclear technologies market, support for the development of Iran's civil nuclear program, and an assured supply of nuclear fuel for Iranian reactors from Russia as well as negotiations for an EU-Iran trade and cooperation agreement and support for Iran's accession to the WTO. Iran, on its part, was expected to make a binding commitment to refrain from uranium conversion, enrichment, and fuel reprocessing for at least ten years, to continue cooperation with the IAEA, to ratify the Additional Protocol by the end of the year, to agree to arrangements for the supply of nuclear fuel from outside Iran and the return of spent fuel, and to make a legally binding commitment not to leave the NPT.

In short, the incentives were rather vague, the demands quite explicit. Rather than accepting the proposal as a basis for further exploration, Iran rejected it immediately. One day later, Mahmoud Ahmadinejad was sworn in as Iran's new president, and, another two days later, Iran restarted uranium conversion (a precursor to enrichment) at a plant in Isfahan. At the IAEA board meeting in September, a European-drafted resolution was passed condemning Iran for noncompliance with the NPT.

One could call this the beginning of a period of robust diplomacy. Iran repeatedly stated its interest to continue negotiations but rejected a renewed suspension of its enrichment-related activities. On the contrary, in January 2006, Iran removed IAEA seals in the enrichment facility in Natanz. In February, the IAEA board of governors responded by referring the case to the UN Security Council where it so far has remained.

Attempts to solve the issue through talks and initiatives have since been accompanied by Security Council action. In May, U.S. Secretary of State Condoleezza Rice announced that Washington was prepared to join the Europeans in talks with Iran once Iran suspended its enrichment. On June 6, 2006, EU foreign policy chief Javier Solana presented to the Iranians a new, more substantive offer that was now explicitly backed by the United States as well as by Russia and China. It reaffirmed as a principle "Iran's inalienable right to nuclear energy for peaceful purposes without discrimination and in conformity with Articles I and II of the NPT." It went beyond the European proposal of 2005 in offering cooperation in the development of a civil nuclear power program, negotiations for a Euratom-Iran nuclear cooperation agreement, and support for the building of light-water reactors in Iran. It demanded a moratorium on Iranian enrichment but implicitly accepted uranium conversion in Iran and foresaw a review of that moratorium once "international confidence in the exclusively peaceful nature of Iran's civil nuclear program has been restored." It also envisaged cooperation in other high-technology fields, an energy partnership between Iran and the EU, and, rather vaguely, "support for a new conference to promote dialogue and cooperation on regional security issues." More specific language, let alone the talk of security guarantees, had been rejected by Washington.

At the same time a Security Council resolution was prepared and passed, the first in a series of resolutions on the matter.[84] It endorsed the offer of June 6, demanding at the same time that Iran suspend its uranium enrichment activities by the end of August and threatening sanctions if Tehran would not comply. The Iranian leadership clearly had no intention of doing so, insisting on its legitimate, "inalienable" rights as NPT member and on a return of the file from the Security Council to the IAEA.

A certain pattern of action developed whereby the five permanent members of the Security Council and Germany, the so-called 3 plus 3 or 5 plus 1 grouping, coordinated Security Council action; Iran pursued the installation of centrifuges in Natanz; and Javier Solana and Iran's chief nuclear negotiator, Ali Larijani, unsuccessfully tried to break the impasse in repeated rounds of talks. In December 2006 and March 2007, two further Security Council resolutions (1737 and 1747) were passed to impose a number of relatively light sanctions on the country, particularly travel restrictions for Iranians involved in the nuclear program and financial freezes on certain Iranian firms and some Revolutionary Guards establishments. In addition to that, the United States had imposed its own financial sanctions on Iran. Washington also put direct pressure on European banks and other companies to reduce or cease their business with Iran. The EU implemented the UN sanctions rather rigorously by adding to the list of persons who would be denied visas.

Iran acted defiantly, claiming that there was no legal basis for a referral to the United Nations Security Council in the first place, let alone for the sanctions. All Iranian nuclear activities were for peaceful purposes and that peaceful program would be speeded up. In April 2007, Iran announced that it now had 3,000 working centrifuges and was able to enrich uranium on an industrial scale.

---

84 "Resolution 1696 (2006)," July 31, 2006, http://daccessdds.un.org/doc/ UNDOC/GEN/N06/450/22/PDF/N0645022.pdf?OpenElement.

Diplomatic attempts to resolve the conflict continued, however. Javier Solana regularly met with Iran's chief negotiator, Ali Larijani. In August, the IAEA outlined a work plan, according to which all remaining issues regarding Iran's past nuclear program and activities should be clarified. In October, Larijani resigned in a conflict with the president over how to handle the nuclear issue. While talks continued between Solana and Larijani's replacement, Saeed Jalili, they became less constructive. The new Iranian representative tended to act more like a spokesman than a negotiator.

In November 2007, the United States released a new NIE on Iran. What made headlines was that it stated "with high confidence" that Iran had halted its nuclear weaponization program in 2003. The estimate also stressed, however, that Iran had been working to develop nuclear weapons up to that time, that it would be able to reverse the decision of 2003, and that "it has the scientific, technical and industrial capacity eventually to produce nuclear weapons if it decides so." The NIE also confirmed an assumption that had been guiding Europe's diplomatic approach to Iran, namely that Tehran's decisions were guided by a calculation of costs and benefits and could therefore be influenced by pressure as well as "opportunities for Iran to achieve its security, prestige, and goals for regional influence in other ways."[85]

An IAEA report of February 2008 that summarized the answers Iran had given in the context of the work plan of August 2007 brought some insights about Iran's past nuclear activities but failed to clarify all outstanding questions. On March 3, 2008, the Security Council passed a third resolution (1803) that tightened existing sanctions by imposing additional travel bans on Iranian individuals and calling for "vigilance" in providing support for trade with Iran and over interactions with Iranian banks. The resolution was accompanied by a statement from the foreign ministers of the five permanent members of the Security Council and Germany restating their commitment to further negotiations on the basis of their 2006 proposal for cooperation. Iran dismissed the resolution, and President Ahmadinejad declared that there was no longer any value in continuing talks with the EU. A nuclear negotiator later explained that Iran would still be prepared to talk about its nuclear program with the West, but only if Western nations would "stop threatening" Iran with further punitive measures.[86]

---

85 "Iran: Nuclear Intentions and Capabilities."

86 Agence France-Presse, March 10, 2008.

Because the NIE had somewhat reduced the urgency of reaching a breakthrough rather soon, Western officials increasingly expressed the feeling that the issue would probably remain unresolved for the time being and still be on the table for the next U.S. president.

Resolution 1803 could well be the last Security Council resolution on the issue, at least for some time. To reach it with near consensus had already been enormously difficult given the uneasiness or resistance on the part of Russia, China, and the nonaligned members of the council. Days after resolution 1803 had been passed in New York, the EU countries had to realize that there was no appetite among most member countries to pass a similar resolution in the IAEA board of governors. The story of negotiations, unofficial talks, and Security Council action beginning in 2003, particularly from 2005 to 2008, seemed to have reached a dead end or a stage, at least, where both sides would be able to continue their individual courses without necessarily advancing their interests.

Over the years, all sides have at different instances been playing for time and have arguably missed opportunities to at least seriously consider initiatives of the other side. Iranian negotiators of the Khatami period repeatedly explained to Iranian audiences that their negotiations with the Europeans allowed the country to complete technical achievements and to win European support against U.S. pressures to refer the issue to the Security Council at that time.[87] Western powers, too, at certain points allowed time to pass in the hope that pressure would work and the political situation in Iran would improve. The United States, as noted, did not respond to the Iranian offer of 2003 that could have been an opportunity to try out Khatami and his intentions. In the spring of 2005, Iran's then chief negotiator Rohani made an initiative toward the EU-3 in order to find an agreement about "objective guarantees" for the peaceful nature of Iran's nuclear program. The Europeans studied it, deemed it interesting at first, but backed off when Washington made clear that it would not support a deal on that basis. Referring to this episode, Iranians have sometimes criticized the Europeans for being "not serious" and not proceeding unless they receive a green light from the United States. At the same time, Iranian negotiators did

---

87 See Bill Samii, "Iran: Former Nuclear Negotiator Remains Committed to National Ambitions," Radio Free Europe, March 7, 2006; see also Bar, Machtiger, and Bachar, "Iranian Nuclear Decision Making under Ahmadinejad," 3, quoting an August 4, 2005, statement on Iranian television by former negotiator Hossein Mosavian.

accept, implicitly at least, that an agreement would eventually need U.S. consent and that Europe would have to bring in the United States. Europeans, however, also played for time at that particular point. When Rohani launched his initiative, President Khatami's second term was reaching its end. Many European (as well as U.S.) diplomats thought that it would be better to wait for and then make a deal with Rafsanjani, who so many expected would win the presidential elections.

The temporary suspension of enrichment, which the Europeans reached through the 2003 and 2004 agreements with Tehran, certainly helped to slow down the Iranian program for that time.[88] From 2005 on, however, the EU seemed be running after the Iranians. Under Khatami, Iranian negotiators had occasionally suggested that Iran be allowed a "laboratory scale" enrichment program. Figures traded amounted to twenty centrifuges at one point, or a cascade of 164 at another. Europeans discussed among them whether, as part of a deal, the West would be prepared to allow Iran at least some of the "enrichment-related" activities, such as uranium conversion. Once Ahmadinejad had taken over, uranium conversion was resumed without an agreement, and the Europeans accepted it as a fact in their internationally backed offer of June 2006. Meanwhile, the number of centrifuges installed in Natanz was increased, and in 2007 the Iranian president announced that Iran was now in the state to produce enriched uranium on an industrial scale. This was likely a gross exaggeration. The cascades were reportedly not working well, but there was no doubt that Iran now had a 3,000-centrifuge capacity. While it still may be possible that Tehran, in order to build or rebuild trust, would at some point decide to pause in operating the cascades in Natanz, it can hardly be expected that it would simply give up this capability.

From an Iranian perspective, cooperation between the EU countries and the United States on the Iranian nuclear file had evolved from an implicit good-cop, bad-cop type of role distribution toward an approach where both Americans and Europeans joined in becoming bad cops. Certainly, the "wall of mistrust" (as Khatami once called it) had become thicker than ever before. Iranian negotiators were, and are, convinced that Washington would not accept any Iranian move, short of regime change, as sufficient to "restore confidence." And, while Iranian officials continue to insist on their right to peaceful nuclear

---

88 See Mark Fitzpatrick, "Can Iran's Nuclear Capability Be Kept Latent?" *Survival* 49, no. 1 (2007): 34.

activities, their European counterparts, and U.S. officials even more so, have increasing doubts about these peaceful intentions. Many if not the majority of Western policymakers and pundits are convinced that Tehran definitely "wants the bomb."

Progress, Status, Security:
The Iranian Elite and National Interests
It may not in fact be all so clear what Tehran really wants. Iran's political elite, as we have seen, are not unified, not even with regard to the nuclear program. There are common denominators though, and there is a common line, namely the constant assertion that the nuclear program has no military purpose. It is interesting that this message is sent equally to foreign and domestic audiences by negotiators and the media, as well as by religious and political leaders at, for example, Friday prayers. In 2004, the *rahbar*, Ayatollah Khamene'i, even issued a fatwa that reportedly rules that Islam prohibits the production, stockpiling, and use of nuclear weapons.[89] Skepticism as to the value of such an edict is certainly in place, particularly given the fact that it seems to never have been published.[90] However, as the Iranian elite has always tried to legitimize policies within an Islamic ideological framework, Khamene'i's ruling about the incompatibility of Islam and atomic weapons is not irrelevant. As one high-ranking diplomat put it to this author, it would be more difficult for an Iranian government to disobey such a fatwa than to violate the NPT.[91] Iranian governments have certainly proved that they can do the latter.

---

89 See BBC Monitoring, August 11, 2004.

90 Fatwas (theological judgments) usually are published in the compilations or, at present, on the Web sites of the scholars who issue them. Khamene'i's statement may not be a fatwa in the strict theological sense; and the exact wording remains unclear. Certainly, a publication of the edict would be a helpful step. More than once Khamene'i has made general statements about the impermissibility of nuclear weapons. An earlier fatwa by senior conservative clerics from Qom that declared nuclear weapons as un-Islamic had been issued in September 2003, at a time when, or shortly before, Iran started to negotiate its nuclear program with the Europeans, signed the Additional Protocol, and, if the 2007 NIE assessment is correct, discontinued its weaponization program. See Bar, Machtiger, and Bachar, "Iranian Nuclear Decision Making under Ahmadinejad," 8.

91 Iranian diplomat, personal communication to author, May 2006.

Although members of the Iranian political elite differ over many issues, they share three beliefs concerning Iran's interests vis-à-vis its international environment. The first is economic and technological progress. The second is status: Iran wants to be recognized as the major regional power. The third, clearly, is security, which for the elite obviously means national as well as regime security. Evidently, the nuclear program bears relevance with respect to each of these elements: nuclear energy is seen as a modern, progressive technology; mastering the fuel cycle is in itself considered proof of great-power status; and even a latent capability to produce a nuclear weapon, if one ever decides so, may be seen, at least by parts of the elite, as a deterrent.[92] The demand for the so-called fuel cycle creates the common basis for those who are simply interested in the scientific and civilian use of nuclear energy, those who want to achieve at least the option of acquiring a military nuclear capability, and those who intend to pursue that option.

With regard to the different factions of the Iranian political elite, we can assume that only parts of what we have called globalists would have been willing to go for the EU-3 offer of August 2005, or even the international offer of June 2006. Neither the Islamo-nationalists nor the realists were prepared to accept these proposals. Islamo-nationalists seem to be intent to at least secure the option of acquiring a military nuclear capacity. They have generally been deeply skeptical with regard to the entire negotiations with Europe and any compromises on Iran's "undeniable rights," and some of their representatives have hinted that Iran might withdraw from the NPT.

For realists like Rafsanjani or Rohani, security is indeed central, and both the 2005 and the 2006 proposals did not contain any convincing security elements, certainly no guarantees against externally forced

92 I tested this thesis (about the three beliefs with regard to Iran's interests) during a roundtable discussion in Tehran in February 2008, where I had been asked to speak about the European perception of developments in Iran. It was interesting to note that participants accepted it as a proper framework for the analysis of the Iranian position, insisting, however, that the Iranian elite were seeking security, not the bomb. George Perkovich of the Carnegie Endowment for International Peace recalled that Rafsanjani once told him: "As long as we can do enrichment and have a mastery of atomic energy, all our neighbors will draw the proper conclusion." See "Dealing with Iran Nuclear Ambitions: What Future Strategy for the International Community?" March 11, 2008, transcript by Federal News Service, Washington, D.C., www.carnegieendowment.org/files/3-11-2008_iranpanel2.pdf.

regime change.[93] We can assume that these realists, with regard to the nuclear program, would ideally keep all options open, including the military one, but they want to avoid their country's international isolation. They also know what a bargain is and would likely be prepared to eventually enter into a deal that would trade Iranian guarantees with regard to its nuclear program with international guarantees for its security. From their perspective a compromise could be possible, not on Iran's "right to the fuel cycle" but on the way to practice this right. At times at least, leaders of this political camp were prepared to consider a ten-year or so suspension of enrichment.[94]

Security may be the most important subject that has to be dealt with for a negotiated resolution of the nuclear conflict with Iran, but the issue of security is also a particularly difficult subject to discuss with Iranian counterparts. Given that Iran insists on the entirely peaceful nature of its program, most officials are reluctant to broach the security issue in the context of a discussion about the nuclear program. They are wary, and probably rightly so, that even a discursive connection between the nuclear issue and the security issue would weaken their argument about the nonmilitary nature of the entire program.

Iranian Motives

Iran's insistence that there was and is no military background to the nuclear program is so unconvincing because so much evidence points in a different direction. Documents about an actual weapons design program, as were presented by IAEA inspectors in March 2008, relate to activities before and up to 2003. Since then, Iran has been cooperating with the IAEA, if not always to the agency's full satisfaction. The way the Iranian nuclear program is designed, however, still strongly suggests an intention to eventually acquire at least the option for a military use, a latent or "breakout" nuclear weapons capability. While there is a logic, even for an oil-rich state like Iran, to set up a nuclear energy program, the actual details of the program do not indicate a purely civilian purpose. Iran will probably not be self-sufficient in uranium, and it would therefore seem more logical to seek international guarantees for

---

93 In their offer of 2005, the EU-3 declared their preparedness to guarantee that Iran would not be attacked by British or French nuclear arms, which is not actually what the Iranian elite fears. The June 2006 offer, as mentioned, spoke of a regional security forum but did not even envisage the possibility of security guarantees.

94 Personal communication, Tehran, May 2006.

long-term fuel delivery or enter into multilateral joint ventures than to insist on an independent enrichment capacity.

The planned heavy-water reactor in Arak would not so much be an efficient installation for power production but could open a plutonium path to nuclear arms. And the history of safeguards violations, various military links to different elements of the program (again probably up to 2003), the inability of Iranian authorities to come clean on that history by giving convincing answers to all IAEA questions in that context, and the continued repeated denials of IAEA inspection visits to certain sites—these all raise further suspicions.[95]

Assessments about the motives for Iran to pursue at least a latent military nuclear capability vary little. Observers differ mainly about the order of priorities in Iranian thinking. Clearly, security is the prime objective: a nuclear capability would be seen as a means of deterrence. Previously, the main threat, certainly the one that triggered the relaunch of the nuclear program in the 1980s, was Iraq. Today some form of deterrence is sought against any possible intention of the United States to attack Iran or enforce regime change.[96] Israel, in contrast, seems to remain rather peripheral in Iran's nuclear calculations.[97] Pakistan is a matter of concern,[98] but it would probably in itself not be sufficient to make Iran invest enormous human and material resources into a program that the international community wants it to abandon.

Above and beyond this defensive dimension, the quest for regional leadership can be seen as an objective. A nuclear capability would increase Tehran's regional and international status and might enable it to block U.S. plans for a reordering of the region that are seen as a threat to the regime or its regional position.[99] Most probably, other actors would be forced to deal with Iran with more respect to its interests.[100]

---

95 See Mark Fitzpatrick, "Is Iran's Nuclear Program Intended Solely for Civilian Purposes?" *Security & Terrorism Research Bulletin,* no. 7 (December 2007): 18–21; Fitzpatrick, "Can Iran's Nuclear Capability Be Kept Latent?" 33–58.

96 See, among others, Kam, *A Nuclear Iran;* and Takeyh, *Hidden Iran,* 221.

97 Dueck and Takeyh, "Iran's Nuclear Challenge," 193.

98 Ibid.

99 Chubin, *Iran's Nuclear Ambitions,* 113–133.

100 Kam, A Nuclear Iran; Tim Guldiman, "The Iranian Nuclear Impasse," *Survival* 49, no. 3 (2007): 176.

Eventually, a nuclear capability might also be useful as a bargaining chip in some form of grand bargain with Washington.[101]

These are all rather rational, realist motives. There is also wide agreement among analysts that Iran's nuclear policy is not determined by ideology. Iran's nuclear weapon, if Tehran were to have one, would not be an "Islamic bomb," but an instrument to safeguard the Islamic Republic's national interest.[102]

Many regional and international observers have little doubt that the Iranian leadership has definitely decided to go for "the bomb." As noted, however, Iran's political elite are not united, not even on the nuclear issue. There are differences within the leadership and the politically relevant elite not only about how to proceed tactically but also how far the nuclear program should, ideally, be driven. Discussions in Iran are not always transparent, but they give clues about intraelite debates and controversies.

We can assume that important parts of the establishment see the question mainly as one of equal rights in a world that tries to deny Iran what others have been allowed. Others remain normatively opposed to nuclear weapons. In contrast with those who see the deterrent value of nuclear arms, some elite members, and not the least important ones, have open doubts that the actual possession of such a weapon would really increase their security. In a crisis situation—over the Strait of Hormuz, for example—the presence or presumed presence of nuclear arms in Iran could indeed draw a decapitation strike by the United States or Israel rather than deter it.[103] Individual Iranian interlocutors also stress that Iran has other, probably more efficient, means of deterrence, including asymmetrical instruments of warfare. To quote one Iranian policy adviser: "Our second-strike capability is not nuclear." This does not, however, mean that they would want to give up the fuel cycle just to surrender to or build confidence with the EU or the 3 plus 3.

Mark Fitzpatrick rightly states that nobody "on the outside knows if Iran has made a decision to produce nuclear weapons."[104] This might not be due to a lack of knowledge about Iranian decision making but rather might reflect an Iranian reality. One cannot ignore that Iran has

---

101 Chubin, *Iran's Nuclear Ambitions*, 137.

102 Dueck and Takeyh, "Iran's Nuclear Challenge," 195.

103 See, among others, Lothat Rühl, "Was will Teheran mit der Bombe?" *Frankfurter Allgemeine Zeitung*, February 16, 2008.

104 Fitzpatrick, "Can Iran's Nuclear Capability Be Kept Latent?" 33.

pursued its fuel cycle program against enormous resistance from the international community. Under Ahmadinejad, Tehran has also been prepared to suffer international sanctions rather than seek a face-saving compromise. By insisting at every possible occasion that the "right to exercise the fuel cycle" is undeniable and will never be given up, the leadership in Tehran may have maneuvered itself into a trap: any compromise could now be seen as compromising on a key aspect of national security.[105] But it is also notable that Iran has not, even under Ahmadinejad, launched a crash program to build a nuclear device in the shortest possible time.[106] If the assessment of the 2007 NIE about the Iranian leadership's 2003 decision to discontinue the weaponization program is correct, we may well assume that this is also the current state of affairs. There are enough domestic and foreign policy reasons for the Iranian leadership to not pursue more than a latent nuclear capability. Iranians would not like to be seen as breaking the NPT openly, and they might not want to have to sort out domestically which agency in the country would eventually be in control not only of different parts of a nuclear program but also of an actual nuclear weapon.

Representatives of the realist camp in Iran, in particular, communicate quite clearly that they want their country to have capabilities similar to those of Japan or Germany, both of which, if they ever decided to, could produce nuclear arms in almost no time. What even Iranian realists do not always easily accept is that the international community, given the different levels of trust that Japan and Iran enjoy internationally (as well as Japan's strict adherence to its obligations under the NPT and the Additional Protocol, and the fact that Japan has no ballistic missile program, and it started to engage in fuel cycle activities only when it already had nuclear reactors), would not want to see Iran in this position.[107]

It is highly probable, therefore, that a definite strategic decision about the ultimate goal of the nuclear program has not been taken yet. Iran's different leadership factions not only might have different views about the program but also will take regional and international developments into consideration, opportunistically rather than as a

---

105   Chubin, *Iran's Nuclear Ambitions.*

106   Dueck and Takeyh, "Iran's Nuclear Challenge."

107   Personal communications with the author, Tehran, February 2008 and earlier.

matter of principle or ideology,[108] and they will weigh the costs and benefits of different paths, particularly with regard to the survival and security of the regime.

Public opinion with regard to the nuclear program is difficult to gauge. Representatives of the political leadership like to state that all Iran is united in its defense of the country's right to operate a nuclear fuel cycle. The few polls that have been conducted by foreign institutes suggest that Iranians, while certainly proud of national technical achievements, are not too eager to pursue a program that would carry a heavy price, particularly in terms of international isolation or confrontation.[109] Anecdotal evidence gives a somewhat mixed picture in that some of the "ordinary" people do not necessarily distinguish between a civilian and a military capacity. One will also hear liberal-minded intellectuals who are no friends of Ahmadinejad define a military nuclear capability as a "legitimate goal."[110]

And If Iran Gets the Bomb?

Two years into the referral of Iran's nuclear file to the Security Council, there cannot be much hope that Tehran would finally give in to diplomatic pressure and abandon its enrichment program. And there is also no guarantee that it will not eventually acquire a military nuclear capability. Although it seems rather unlikely that Iran, under current circumstances, would proceed farther than achieving a latent nuclear capability, one cannot exclude a scenario whereby Tehran would overstep the nuclear threshold. It could either openly break the NPT by declaring itself a (military) nuclear power and parading or even exploding a nuclear device, or it could follow Israel's example of nuclear ambiguity—it would then acquire nuclear weapons, but it would neither announce this nor conduct any tests, relying instead on the deterrent value of being considered a nuclear-armed state, and not denying what others suppose.[111]

What would be the main implications of a nuclear Iran? Primarily, there would be more uncertainty in the entire region. Israel would, for the first time in its existence, be in a situation in which a hostile country

---

108 Chubin, *Iran's Nuclear Ambitions.*

109 See Guldiman, "The Iranian Nuclear Impasse," 177 n. 5.

110 Personal interviews, Tehran and Isfahan, 2006.

111 On these different options see particularly Kam, *A Nuclear Iran.*

could strike it a critical blow. And while Israel could decide that it was able to live with the threat, it could still panic.[112]

The nuclear status as such would not turn regional power relations on their head. Given its size, its material and human resources, and its influence in other countries in the region, Iran already is the leading power in the Persian Gulf and, with Israel and Turkey, one of the leading powers in the wider region. Iran could feel itself less deterred, however, from using its influence and resources in an assertive or aggressive manner and pursue activities with regard to Iraq, the GCC states, or the Mashreq that hitherto would have been seen as too risky. Iran could give more support to Hezbollah in Lebanon and Hamas in the Palestinian territories or theoretically even offer a shield of nuclear deterrence to Syria.[113] One might legitimately ask what kind of concessions, for example, Tehran actually could press from its Arab neighbors in the Persian Gulf if it had a nuclear weapon that it could not get from them by means of the instruments of power it already has at its disposal. Nuclear weapons alone do not provide political influence.[114] You cannot impose, say, a friendly government in Baghdad or end the discrimination of Shiites in Bahrain by threatening to use a nuclear bomb. Undoubtedly, however, the impression exists among the regional states and societies that Iran, with a bomb, would achieve a more dominant regional position than it already has. Certainly, smaller states in the region could feel the need to bandwagon with Iran. Others would probably, if hesitantly, seek to build an Arab alliance with strong defensive links to the United States. Such a polarization would not bode well for the prospects of regional cooperation, neither in the economic field nor with regard to solving regionalized domestic conflicts such as, currently, those in Iraq or Lebanon.

The prospect of such a development could encourage other states in the region to seek a similar status. In December 2006, the GCC announced that it would establish a joint nuclear research program. Aside from the economic rationale of saving oil and gas for exports and using nuclear energy for desalination and energy production, the decision to launch such a program, as well as the decisions of individual GCC states to initial agreements with France for the purchase of nuclear power sta-

---

112 Ibid., 49, 57.

113 Ibid., 59.

114 Christoph Bertram, *Partner, nicht Gegner: Für eine andere Iran-Politik* (Hamburg: Körber-Stiftung, 2008 [forthcoming]).

tions, was clearly seen, and was meant to be seen, as a response to the Iranian program, as a signal that, if the international community failed to stop Iran from acquiring a military nuclear capability, the GCC states could also opt for a military program.[115] One may again doubt whether such a response would be realistic at all, given that political costs and material difficulties of going nuclear have increased and Arab states that feel threatened by Iran could more easily choose to enter into a defense alliance with the United States.[116] The feeling in the region is a different one, namely, that even states like Egypt, Turkey, Saudi Arabia, and others, which have no intention of acquiring nuclear weapons at the moment, could reconsider their positions if Iran were to acquire a nuclear military capability.[117] The primary motive would be to match the status of Iran. One need not assume that this would immediately lead to an arms race, but political pressures inside these countries could mount, and a state like Syria, seeking deterrence against Israel, could try to test the rigidity of an already weakened nonproliferation regime. There is no doubt that the NPT would lose credibility if Iran were able to become a military nuclear power. The IAEA would seriously be weakened.[118]

There is wide agreement, even among Israeli analysts who obviously give the question highest importance, that Iran would not pass

---

115 Nicole Stracke, "Nuclear Development in the Gulf: A Strategic or Economic Necessity?" *Security & Terrorism Research Bulletin,* no. 7 (2007): 5.

116 Bertram, *Partner, nicht Gegner.*

117 See among others Mustafa Alani, "Nuclear Terrorism in the Gulf: Myth or Reality?" *Security & Terrorism Research Bulletin,* no. 7 (2007): 13; Pedatzur, "The Iranian Nuclear Threat and the Israeli Options," 520; Ian O. Lesser, "Turkey, Iran and Nuclear Risks," in *Getting Ready for a Nuclear-Ready Iran,* ed. Henry D. Sokolski and Patrick Clawson (Washington, D.C.: Strategic Studies Institute, 2005), 104.

118 There have already been suggestions that an independent technical commission should be established by the Security Council to investigate the Iranian nuclear program independently from the IAEA, that is, sidelining the agency; see Efraim Asculai, "Can We Rely on the IAEA?" INSS Policy Brief, no. 9 (December 27, 2007). The fact that this suggestion here comes from an Israeli scholar may lead some observers to dismiss it as another element of the conflict between Israel and Iran. This would be unwise; the suggestion could easily be taken up by members of the Security Council whose confidence in international organizations is limited in the first place.

nuclear arms to Hezbollah or terrorist organizations, and that it would not use its nuclear arms to attack Israel unless, perhaps, the Iranian regime was itself existentially threatened.[119] Iranian leaders are aware that a nuclear attack on Israel would draw the most severe response from Israel itself as well as from the United States, and they would not use their capacities in a suicidal manner "simply to kill Zionist infidels."[120] Israel would maintain a second-strike capability, and Iran itself would remain deterrable.

Iran's main gain would indeed be deterrence, particularly with regard to U.S. or Israeli plans to seek regime change in Tehran through an attack on the country. One Israel scholar assumes that eventually a Middle Eastern form of mutual assured destruction would emerge between Israel and Iran.[121] This may well be so, even though there would be a high risk of miscalculation for quite some time. Actors in the Middle East have no common experience with a situation of nuclear confrontation, no reliable lines of communication, little knowledge about the others' redlines, no guarantees that the actors would understand one another, and no code of conduct that could help to defuse critical situations. Of course, it is also possible that Iran, having assured deterrence but knowing about the risks of nuclear miscalculation, would itself act more cautiously, as was the case with Pakistan and India. This, however, is nothing one could rely upon.[122]

Eventually Western and other states would probably react to a nuclear-armed Iran with a policy of strong deterrence and different grades of engagement or détente, which would include offers to talk and to cooperate whenever and to the extent to which Tehran's behavior would allow for such engagement. This would likely include all kinds of efforts to establish regional and bilateral security arrangements or "management regimes" about, for instance, maritime security or the prevention of incidents at sea.[123] Nothing of this is wrong. It might

---

119 Kam, *A Nuclear Iran,* 50 ff.

120 Pedatzur, "The Iranian Nuclear Threat and the Israeli Options," 535.

121 Ibid., 536.

122 For the entire argument see Kam, *A Nuclear Iran,* 50 ff.

123 See Henry Sokolski, "Getting Ready for a Nuclear-Ready Iran: Report of the NPEC Working Group," and Douglas E. Streusand, "Managing the Iranian Threat to Sea Commerce Diplomatically," in *Getting Ready for a Nuclear-Ready Iran,* ed. Sokolski and Clawson, 1–19 and 257–284, respectively.

be easier to reach, however, if such efforts were started as long as the nuclear-breakout scenario of Iran has not materialized.

Iran, Europe, the United States, or Where Do We Go from Here?

There is no simple foolproof strategy for solving conflicts between Iran and the international community and eventually reaching stability and peace in the Persian Gulf region. Steps and measures for the immediate future have to be distinguished from policies for the middle and long term, and different lines of action may have to be followed in parallel. Many relevant actors have to play their roles, not only the United States and Iran themselves. With some analytical simplification we can say that the problem is one of security and trust: on one level, security for Iran and international trust in Iran's intentions, and, on a second level, security for Iran's neighborhood and Iranian trust in the international community.

Writing from a European perspective, this author naturally concentrates primarily on the role of the EU, the United States, and the international community represented by the 3 plus 3 that have acted as the main interlocutors for Iran and have prepared and largely determined Security Council action. Recommendations here are influenced by a pragmatic, realist approach. This means basically that for a sound management of international relations and in order to reach sustainable solutions to international conflicts, the interests of all relevant stakeholders will have to be considered. While some interests of some states or regimes may be illegitimate, all states have legitimate interests. The task of diplomacy is to accommodate these interests in a way that at least helps to build international peace and security.

Success is, of course, only one possible outcome. Others are possible. Javier Solana, however, was right when he stated, with regard to the nuclear conflict with Iran, that a solution would eventually have to be built on a negotiated outcome.[124]

While this manuscript is being finished in spring 2008, the combination of pressure, diplomatic initiatives, and talks will probably continue for some time. It is unlikely that any breakthrough in the attempts to

---

124 Javier Solana (remarks [S274/06] to the European Parliament Foreign Affairs Committee, October 4, 2006), www.consilium.europa.eu/ueDocs/cms_Data/docs/pressdata/en/discours/91168.pdf.

solve the issue can be achieved before, at the very best, the fall of 2009. In the first months of 2009, a new U.S. president will be busy with getting his appointments confirmed by Congress and will probably start with a foreign policy review before undertaking major new foreign policy steps. Then in the summer, there will be presidential elections in Iran. Although his position has been weakened, Western governments should not rule out the possibility of President Ahmadinejad winning a second mandate. It may then be the task of the new, or the reelected, Iranian president to set out for a new beginning with the United States.

Sanctions

Even then, this will hardly come about easily, and the road to such an endeavor may be mined with mutual accusations, threats, and dangerous incidents. It is also unlikely that UN Security Council sanctions that have been imposed on Iran would be rescinded as long as stalemate continues. Certainly, the offer of "dual suspension" should be maintained. If Iran were to pause in the operation of its enrichment program, sanctions would also be suspended.

It should also be clear that sanctions are not meant to cripple the Iranian economy, nor to enforce regime change, and not even to punish Iran for its long-term violation of NPT safeguards in the past. Obviously, it is politically very difficult for the Iranian leadership to lay open the details of a nuclear program that almost everybody else in the world believes had a military purpose, at least up to 2003. The threat that new sanctions might be imposed if such a military dimension, even in the past, was eventually to be proven does also not give an incentive to reveal it. To rebuild trust, however, it would be necessary for Iran to come clean on these aspects. The international community might want to help the Iranian leadership to do so through a declaration of the Security Council or the IAEA board of governors to the effect that any voluntary disclosure by Iran of previously clandestine nuclear activities would be considered as an active measure of confidence building.[125]

Any sanctions should come in the context of a perspective, an offer that Iran finds attractive enough and will not refuse in the end. Currently, the European and Western strategies are not clear. Neither are sanctions that have been imposed by the Security Council particularly

---

125 This has been proposed by Pierre Goldschmidt; for details, see his "Verifying Iran's Nuclear Program: Is the International Community Up to the Task?" (Lamont Lecture, Belfer Center, Harvard University, October 30, 2007).

heavy, nor is the engagement offer clear and attractive enough in that it would expressly indicate the preparedness of the United States for recognizing and respecting the legitimacy of the Islamic Republic. Any new sanctions aiming at a change of Iranian behavior should be clear and should be agreed upon in the Security Council, demonstrating to the Iranian public that Iran indeed has a conflict with the international community, not with individual Western states. This is both a question of legitimacy and of the political impact in Iran.

U.S. policymakers have occasionally demanded that Europe impose its own bilateral sanctions on Iran so as to curb trade and other business relations between Europe and Iran. Both politically and economically, this does not make too much sense. While certainly hurting European business interests, such unilateral measures do not commit any state outside the EU and only create further trade diversion.[126] Sanctions also should not undermine the prospects for regional cooperation in the Middle East. Common energy infrastructure projects—between Turkey and Iran, or Iran, Pakistan and India, for example—will have a stabilizing and confidence-building effect. Given the relative lightness of the measures that the Security Council has taken so far, the international community might rather consider a more robust but more targeted form of sanctions, namely an arms embargo. If imposed by the Security

---

126 For U.S. politicians, it may of course still make sense to demand that Europe impose its own stricter trade sanctions. It demonstrates international pressure on Iran, and it does not cost the U.S. economy anything. On the contrary, U.S. firms may be in a better position to step in in the future, once sanctions are lifted, if European companies reduce or give up their business relationship with Iran today. It is also understandable, therefore, that European business associations and policymakers are somewhat skeptical with regard to such demands from the U.S. side. European policymakers have occasionally pointed out to their U.S. colleagues that some U.S. firms are quite active in Iran: Iranian construction companies might get their Caterpillar trucks from the Swiss subsidiary of the U.S. firm, but it is still a Caterpillar truck. This is not illegal sanctions busting because U.S. firms can get waivers from their administration and thereby legally work in Iran through their foreign subsidiaries. Iranians, of course, are happy to see the new Tehran airport being equipped with GE technology, to contact Halliburton through the Halliburton office on Kish Island, or to drink Coca-Cola (the license for the production of the brown beverage is indirectly held by the Imam-Reza *bonyad*).

Council, it could make a difference in the Iranian calculation.[127] The general principle here should be that if costs rise through sanctions or the threat of sanctions, opportunities and gains for Iran would also have to increase if it takes a different course. This has to include a serious perspective of security, cooperation, and partnership.

Strategic Transparency

The period ahead may thus be one of stalemate and mutual blockade; however, it could also be used by Iran, the United States, Europe, and others to think about or rethink their respective strategies, as well as to build or rebuild some trust. Transparency about each party's respective goals and interests could be part of such confidence-building efforts.

European interests and goals with regard to the Persian Gulf region are quite clear: Europe has a vital interest in regional stability. This implies the right of all states in the region to live in security, regardless of the nature of the individual regimes. Regional peace and stability will also enhance the chances for peaceful political development. Europe also has a strong interest in preventing nuclear proliferation. Rhetorically at least, Iran and the West are not far apart here. Iran, after all, constantly claims that it has no intention of acquiring a bomb. Europe also seeks a partnership with the region that ideally includes all states and societies and comprises security, political, economic, environmental, and development dimensions. It would need to help regional states and societies achieve their developmental and technological ambitions and make best use of the natural resources of the region. Iran has a special place here. It could indeed become a main partner for Europe in the region, in a partnership with multiple and partly strategic dimensions. Partnership, of course, demands that all would-be partners have to deliver inputs.

Central Role of the United States

Different international players have different roles in this story. Despite deep mutual mistrust there will be no solution to the conflict, or rather the conflicts, between Iran and the international community without the involvement of the United States. As noted earlier, there are certain Iranian interests that only Washington would be able to respond to in a convincing way. Washington therefore has a central role.

---

127 Goldschmidt, "Verifying Iran's Nuclear Program."

It is almost as much in the interest of the United States as in that of regional states and societies and of the international community to avoid a military conflict with Iran. To keep the threat of a military strike on the table is one thing that should not be excluded in the context of a robust diplomacy; to actually execute it is quite a different thing. The Middle East is already overburdened with conflicts that could easily explode and develop into military confrontations between states, between states and nonstate actors, or between confessional or ethnic militias. The region does not need one more war. Military strikes on Iranian nuclear facilities are certainly possible, and they would likely set Iran's nuclear program back for a couple of years. Any military escalation, however, is likely to achieve results the United States itself wants to avoid.[128]

This is not the place to develop scenarios for what a military campaign against Iran would lead to. What is certain, though, is that chain reactions that could involve the Strait of Hormuz; the smaller Persian Gulf countries; and Iraq, Lebanon, Syria, Palestine, and Israel would not be controllable. War with Iran would also not improve the image of the United States and the West in the region, except, perhaps, among some of the elites of some of the Gulf Arab countries. On the contrary, the hostility of large parts of the societies in the Arab and Muslim world would only increase.

For the short term, Washington would be well advised to avoid aggressive rhetoric that usually only strengthens hard-liners in Tehran. Even in the absence of normal relations, U.S. policymakers should treat their Iranian counterparts with respect. If Washington eventually wants to reach a satisfactory outcome with Tehran, there is no reason to try to delegitimize Khamene'i as an "unelected decision maker." Khamene'i is in charge, as much as Mao Zedong and Leonid Brezhnev were in their time. And in spite of the frequent manipulations of Iranian elections, Iranian leaders generally have more democratic legitimacy than most other leaders in the Middle East.

Washington will not like it, but the strengthened position of Tehran in the Persian Gulf region is a fact, and it has to be acknowledged as such. It is there even without a military nuclear capability, and largely so as a result of the U.S.-led war against Iraq. In the short term, the United

---

128 See Sam Gardiner, "The End of the 'Summer of Diplomacy': Assessing U.S. Military Options on Iran" (New York: The Century Foundation, 2006), www.tcf.org/publications/internationalaffairs/gardiner_summer_diplomacy.pdf.

States would be well advised to continue and intensify its intermittent, limited dialogue with Iran, whether on the ambassadorial level in Baghdad or on a more elevated level in the multilateral format of the Iraq Neighbors conferences. As noted earlier, Iran and the United States have overlapping interests in Iraq. They both essentially want Iraq to be stable, they want the Iraqi government to establish its authority, and they both even want a democratic Iraq. Washington needs to realize, however, that Iran will eventually use its influence in Iraq in a consistent way serving its own longer-term interests of stability in Iraq only if its leadership does not feel threatened from the United States. Otherwise, Tehran prefers to have the United States occupied in Iraq instead of thinking about how to use its resources to seek regime change in Tehran. To defuse tension in the Persian Gulf per se, Washington should also try to agree with Iran on a very limited, navy-to-navy agreement about incidents at sea.

A more comprehensive dialogue will probably fall upon the U.S. administration succeeding that of George W. Bush. That dialogue is necessary, however. Talks that are restricted to the Iraqi situation, or indirectly led through the Europeans, will neither bring the real issues between the two countries on the table nor link them. U.S. policymakers will also, to put it in the words of three U.S. scholars, have to relieve themselves of the notion that a diplomatic process with Iran, and eventually the normalization of relations, would be "a concession to the mullahs." Iranian leaders like Ahmadinejad are interested in such a process, not least because it could boost their domestic popularity. Rather than strengthening autocratic tendencies, however, a normalization of Iran's relations with the United States may eventually contribute to the opening up and liberalizing of Iran.[129]

If we correctly assume that Iran's nuclear program has a strong security dimension, then a U.S.-Iranian dialogue, and U.S. policies toward Iran, would have to "diminish Iran's strategic anxieties."[130] No power but the United States is able to address the security concerns

---

129 See Michael McFaul, Abbas Milani, and Larry Diamond, "A Win-Win U.S. Strategy for Dealing with Iran," *Washington Quarterly* 30, no. 1 (2006/2007): 127; Bernd W. Kubbig, *Internationale Sanktionen gegen den Iran: Erfolgsbedingungen und Effektivität,* with Sven-Eric Fikenscher, HSFK Report no. 4/2007 (Frankfurt a.M.: Hessische Stiftung Friedens- und Konfliktforschung [HSFK], 2007), 35, www.hsfk.de/fileadmin/ downloads/report0407_01.pdf.

130 Takeyh, *Hidden Iran,* 223.

of Iran. For the Iranian elite this includes the territorial integrity of the country as much as regime security. As long as the regime feels targeted and not accepted as a legitimate player, it is very unlikely to make the clear decisions with regard to its nuclear program that are needed to rebuild trust with the international community. In a sense, as Shahram Chubin put it, the United States needs to choose between nonengagement and nonproliferation.[131] A policy of anti-Iranian alliance building, as President Bush tried to sell during his Middle East tour in the beginning of 2008, may therefore be exactly the wrong thing to do and another misjudgment of regional dynamics in the Middle East on the part of the Bush administration. Instead, even if it were not to lead to such endeavors, the United States should actively support regional and international efforts to establish inclusive regional security arrangements. It would also be helpful if Washington were to give up its opposition to regional integration projects such as the planned Iran-Pakistan-India gas pipeline or links between Iran's gas fields and Turkey's pipeline system.

Bilaterally, Washington could announce its preparedness to lift certain unilateral sanctions it has imposed on Iran in exchange for goodwill gestures and measures from the Iranian side. Incremental steps of this sort will at best help to improve the atmosphere, however. At some point, Washington will have to make "an offer that Iran cannot refuse."[132] From the U.S. side this could include the reestablishment of full diplomatic relations, the unfreezing of Iranian assets in the United States, and encouragement of U.S. direct investment in Iran, and it would have to eventually include the prospect of some form of security guarantees. Washington would not even have to promise or guarantee what the Bush administration did with regard to North Korea,[133] a state after all that did leave the NPT, has produced nuclear weapons, and tested a nuclear bomb.[134]

---

131 Chubin, *Iran's Nuclear Ambitions,* 142.

132 McFaul, Milani, and Diamond, "A Win-Win U.S. Strategy for Dealing with Iran," 126.

133 Pyongyang was assured in writing that the United States had "no intention to attack or invade the DPRK with nuclear or conventional weapons." See U.S. Department of State, Office of the Spokesman, "Joint Statement of the Fourth Round of the Six-Party Talks," Beijing, September 19, 2005.

134 See the comparison of the Iranian and the North Korean case in Hitoshi

We do not know whether such an offer would convince Iran to give up the suspicious parts of its nuclear program. But both the North Korean and the Libyan cases suggest that security guarantees have helped to achieve diplomatic breakthroughs. Arguably, the Libyan decision of 2003 to give up the country's nuclear weapons program was at least partly due to "a credible [U.S.] offer of regime security."[135] And any offer of security guarantees would be conditional on Iranian moves, not least such elements as Iran seems to have been prepared to offer on its own initiative of May 2003. Primarily this includes the acceptance of an Israel-Palestine two-state solution, the cessation of support for Palestinian militants, and full transparency about Iran's past and current nuclear programs. Deliberations about such mutual offers could become the basis for a "grand bargain" with Iran that is increasingly being discussed in U.S. policy circles.[136]

Europe: The Tasks of Practical Cooperation

Europe will have to continue its role as the main interlocutor with Iran for some time but be prepared that this will be taken over by Washington at some point. Rather than trying to maintain its privileged position here, Europe should actively encourage Washington and Tehran to seek an open and comprehensive dialogue. There is no need to fear that Europe would lose. European states and the EU will still be "in business," economically as well as politically, even after a possible normalization of U.S.-Iran relations. With regard to security issues, the United States, if such a rapprochement comes about, will naturally be the central counterpart for Iran. Europe simply does not have the same influence, presence, and hard power in the Persian Gulf region. Iran, however, as other states in the region, will always be interested in diversified relations. Iran's interaction with the international community will increase in absolute terms, and European companies have

---

Tanaka's contribution to this volume.

135 Robert S. Litwak, *Regime Change: U.S. Strategy through the Prism of 9/11* (Washington, D.C.: Woodrow Wilson Center Press; Baltimore: Johns Hopkins University Press, 2007), 194–199, 290.

136 See particularly Flynt Leverett, "All or Nothing: The Case for a U.S.-Iranian 'Grand Bargain'" (statement to the Subcommittee on National Security and Foreign Affairs, Committee on Oversight and Government Reform, U.S. House of Representatives, November 7, 2007); and William Luers, Thomas R. Pickering, and Jim Walsh, "A Solution for the U.S.-Iran Nuclear Standoff," *New York Review of Books* 55, no. 4 (2008).

multiple advantages in the Iranian market owing not only to Europe's geographic proximity.

Europe should lay out the prospects of, and the conditions for, a multidimensional partnership with Iran and encourage Iran to do the same. One could call that a partnership with strategic dimensions, notably energy,[137] economic development, and science and technology as well as certain aspects of domestic and regional security. No other state in the Persian Gulf region and the Middle East has the same potential. In the long run, Iran with its human and natural resources, its long tradition of urbanization, its civic culture, and its geopolitical position would be the natural regional partner for Europe. Given the unresolved nuclear conflict, however, and Iran's destructive role with regard to the Arab-Israeli conflict and peace process, such a partnership will not materialize in a short time, if it ever does. It is nonetheless useful to be aware of the potential and of the benefits that such a relationship could garner. In the meantime, some confidence can be built through practical cooperation. Among other things, pilot projects on drug enforcement and border control in provinces close to the Afghanistan border should be actively pursued. Iran has an enormous problem with the inflow of drugs from Afghanistan and drug use in its own country. Europe and Iran have a common interest in curbing the illegal drug trade.

Generally, Europe should keep engaging Iran and even increase its engagement, not only on the nuclear file, but also on regional issues and other subjects of common interest. Interparliamentary dialogues can be particularly useful. Such exchanges of members of national parliaments or the European Parliament with members of the Iranian *majlis* are a chance to broach even controversial issues—the state of human rights in Iran, Europe's vital interest in a peaceful solution of the Arab-Israeli conflict, or nonproliferation, to name but a few—with a part of the wider political elite in Iran. Dialogues between parliamentarians, as well as between the think-tank and university communities, help develop an understanding of domestic developments in Iran, and they also are a legitimate means of support to those members of the elite who want to remain connected to the world.

Europe, as noted before, will not play a main role for regional security in the Persian Gulf region. Because Europe, in contrast with

137 For a number of detailed proposals for Iranian-European energy cooperation, see Abbas Maleki, "Energy Supply and Demand in Eurasia: Cooperation between EU and Iran," *China and Eurasia Forum Quarterly* 5, no. 4 (2007): 103–113.

the United States, is not suspected of harboring its own hegemonic aspirations for the region, it can facilitate exchanges between regional actors to explore ideas and possibilities for regional security cooperation. Such exchanges could also broach the issue of what strategic consequences a spread of nuclear arms in the region actually would have for all states.

Europeans should also actively try to establish channels of communication between Israel and Iran. This would be useful at any rate, not only in case Iran eventually becomes a military nuclear power. Currently, Israelis and Iranians do not know from one another where their redlines are or what they consider existential threat levels. To avoid any miscalculation, however, members of the military and political establishments of both states need to understand the strategic calculations of the respective other side.

Europe has never cut off its lines of communication with Iran, and it is good that European actors, despite the difficulties and the sterility of some exchanges, have kept and will keep talking with Iran. Eventually, particularly if Europe was again to present a major offer on behalf of the 3 plus 3, it should find a way to engage the spiritual leader, Ayatollah Khamene'i. He, not the president or the secretary of the National Security Council, will have to take any strategic decision. Of all the world leaders, however, only President Vladimir V. Putin of Russia has so far met him. If Europe wants to bring its message across unfiltered, one or more of its representatives should speak to Khamene'i directly.

Common Tasks

The EU and the United States do not act alone with regard to Iran, and they should not. Neither do they represent the "international community" that we, this author included, refer to so often. Coordination with Russia and China and with the nonpermanent members of the Security Council is essential. Some states outside the 3 plus 3 should be encouraged to play a more active role. South Africa, in particular, should be brought in. As a major nonaligned country and a leading power on its own continent, South Africa enjoys great respect in Tehran. Because Pretoria has voluntarily given up its own military nuclear program, it could be a particularly credible partner in further efforts to negotiate with Iran about its nuclear program. It also clearly understands that any proposal to Iran will need to demonstrate respect for Iran's quest for "independence" and for its "rights." Iran will certainly be prepared to accept and act upon its obligations only if its rights are explicitly acknowledged.

Negotiating Iranian Enrichment

Ideally, the IAEA, the EU-3, or a new contact group that would comprise the current 3 plus 3 and South Africa (making it, in effect, a 5 plus 2 grouping, that is, the five permanent members of the Security Council plus Germany and South Africa) would reach an agreement with Iran, whereby Tehran's technological achievement would be acknowledged—which should be done anyway—and Iran would voluntarily forgo indigenous uranium enrichment and plutonium separation. Such an agreement would need to be globalized, that is, it would have to be endorsed by the Security Council and declared an international model, whereby states that forgo such activities would be guaranteed the provision of nuclear fuel at attractive conditions.[138] This would give new meaning to the NPT. It may not be in the cards for the time being, however.

Given the lack of trust between Iran and the international community, the international demand for a suspension of enrichment activities until such trust is reestablished is legitimate. Since 2006, under Security Council resolution 1737 Iran has even been legally obliged to comply with that demand. Such a moratorium, however, is a goal. It must not be made a condition for comprehensive negotiations.

Realistically, Iran is unlikely to give up the right to and the option of independent enrichment and enrichment-related activities. Iran is also likely to further defy the Security Council, at least as long as the current Iranian administration is in power.

The 3 plus 3 and the Security Council have repeatedly stated that they respect Iran's rights as a member of the NPT to nuclear development, research, and production and that the moratorium demanded from Iran is to be temporary, until trust is reestablished. The Iranian side, on its part, suspects that the international community, and particularly the United States, will forever deny that trust has been rebuilt and thereby force upon Iran an indefinite suspension of its program. It would therefore be helpful to depoliticize the issue, or delink it, as it were, from questions relating to the nature of the regime in Tehran.

---

138 George Perkovich, "Iran Is Not an Island: A Strategy to Mobilize the Neighbors," *Policy Brief* no. 34 (Washington, D.C.: Carnegie Endowment for International Peace, February 2005), 6.

For new negotiations, the 3 plus 3 or a 5 plus 2 grouping should try to determine what guarantees, safeguards, controls, and disclosures would be required from Iran, short of regime change, to make the international community accept independent Iranian research and development on the nuclear fuel cycle. This list would at the minimum have to include the ratification of the Additional Protocol and a disclosure of past activities that most probably have served military purposes. Iranian interlocutors may not like that list, but it could give a positive signal that a suspension will not be forever.

For the international community, there may ultimately be only second-best options. Different proposals are on the table. They basically agree that, rather than demanding zero enrichment, the aim of the international community should be to reach an understanding about limitations on independent Iranian fuel cycle activities, maximum safeguards, and an integration of the Iranian program into a multilateral format.[139] None of these proposals may be perfect. Their beauty lies in the fact that Iran could probably accept them. Pragmatists at least would be interested in exploring them as a way to reintegrate Iran with the world.

Limitations of the program could include a stretching out over time of the development of enrichment-related activities as well as limitations in scope, such as to laboratory-scale activities. Safeguards would involve the ratification of the Additional Protocol by the Iranian Parliament and probably some other measures to be agreed on with the IAEA. A multilateral or international integration of Iran's nuclear activities would serve the dual purpose of allowing Iran access to state-of-the-art technologies and at the same time reduce the fears of neighbors and other states that such technologies would be used for other than peaceful purposes.

What has to be explored in particular is the idea of a multilateral consortium or joint venture for research and industrial-scale production of nuclear fuel. It would have to involve Iran as a full and probably a founding partner. It would allow Iran to fully participate with its partners in research, development, and production, but also reduce the risks

---

139 See, among others, "Iran: Is There a Way Out of the Nuclear Impasse?" *Middle East Report,* no. 51 (Brussels, Washington, Tehran: International Crisis Group, February 23, 2006); Kubbig, *Internationale Sanktionen gegen den Iran,* 34; recently also Luers, Pickering, and Walsh, "A Solution for the U.S.-Iran Nuclear Standoff"; and Gareth Evans, "The Right Nuclear Red Line," *Washington Post,* December 5, 2007.

of diversion or of the production of highly enriched uranium. In 2007, Saudi Arabia proposed the establishment of a regional enrichment and processing consortium for the Middle East that would be under IAEA supervision and located in a country outside the region.[140] International actors should certainly encourage Iran and other regional countries to explore this idea in detail; discussions about the proposal could be a confidence-building measure by themselves. One other option could be to offer Iran membership in, or a partnership with, the British-Dutch-German joint venture Urenco that has the exclusive right to produce low-enriched uranium in these countries and can serve as an example to demonstrate that even industrially developed countries have delegated their "enrichment sovereignty."[141] Former U.S. under secretary of state Thomas Pickering and others have suggested a second-best option whereby a multinational consortium could actually manage enrichment activities in Iran.[142] This is certainly a midterm option, even though it may not be acceptable in the short term to the United States. To achieve a truly multinational format and increase safeguards against any misuse, partners to such a consortium should consider breaking up the fuel cycle into its phases—conversion, enrichment, fuel-rod production, reprocessing—and implementing these different phases in different countries with scientists from all participant states. Politically, this would create a form of collective interdependence that does not limit the sovereignty of any participant but increases the security of all. It could also be considered a test for cooperation and the building of trust.

International Dimension
The Iranian nuclear program and conflict have alerted the world to some of the inherent risks of a spread of nuclear energy. As more and more countries develop an interest in nuclear power, and many of these countries are part and parcel of unstable geopolitical environments, the risk of proliferation also increases. Iran will likely not remain the

---

140 Stracke, "Nuclear Development in the Gulf: A Strategic or Economic Necessity?" 10.

141 Urenco was set up in 1971. The terms of the 1970 Almelo Treaty, which governs the Urenco partnership, prohibit any partner in the group from enriching uranium outside the group.

142 Luers, Pickering, and Walsh, "A Solution for the U.S.-Iran Nuclear Standoff."

only state that, in this respect, causes headaches to the international community.

How to deal with this challenge extends beyond the scope of this study (and the expertise of this author). Suffice it to say here that it is necessary to strengthen the nonproliferation regime. Experts have proposed, among other things, new legislation by the UN Security Council that would ensure effective measures against any state withdrawing from the NPT after having been found to be in noncompliance with its safeguards agreements and that would make the suspension of sensitive fuel cycle activities mandatory on any noncompliant state.[143] It is also necessary to limit the spread of enrichment activities globally and, at the same time, guarantee fuel supply to any state that intends to use nuclear energy. Ideally, no state would operate a nuclear fuel cycle independently. Even if that seems out of reach for the time being, some multilateral arrangements need to be put in place on the way and not only talked about. The prime responsibility for such initiatives certainly lies with the permanent members of the Security Council, but other states could and should be supportive. The United States has pledged an initial $50 million for a fuel bank project if other states commit matching funds. The EU, or individual European states, Japan, Russia, and China as well as the GCC states should follow suit. Iran, on its part, could contribute to building confidence by also pledging funds for this purpose. One more far-reaching, sensible option is an international enrichment center and nuclear fuel bank that would be run by a private consortium and supervised, or even directly managed and owned, by the IAEA.[144] The IAEA governing board should give the go-ahead for the director general of the agency to commission a feasibility study and start talks with countries prepared to host such a facility, preferably neutral countries such as Switzerland, Finland, or Australia.

---

143 See Pierre Goldschmidt, "Priority Steps to Strengthen the Nonproliferation Regime," Nonproliferation Program Policy Outlook (Washington, D.C.: Carnegie Endowment for International Peace, February 2007), 3.

144 For details on the different proposals that have been made in this respect, see Harald Müller, *Multilateralisierung des Brennstoffkreislaufs: Ein Ausweg aus den Nuklearkrisen?* HSFK Report no. 10/2006 (Frankfurt a.M.: Hessische Stiftung Friedens- und Konfliktforschung [HSFK], 2006),

Middle East and Regional Security in the Persian Gulf

We should not forget that the nuclear conflict with Iran is only one aspect, although it is a principal aspect, of instability and insecurity in the Persian Gulf region and the Middle East. Let us start with a mantra here, but an important one that may be restated: Iranian influence on radical organizations in the Palestinian territories, and even in Lebanon, would best be curbed through serious and consistent efforts by the United States and Europe for a fair settlement of the Israeli-Palestinian conflict. Iran is in Palestine mainly by default, filling the void that the United States and Europe have left in many respects through their failure to demonstrate evenhandedness in dealing with both sides to the conflict, to talk to political forces that won democratic elections, or to prevent a humanitarian catastrophe in the Gaza Strip. With a "just and lasting peace" (as the formula goes) that would allow the two states of Israel and Palestine to live side by side in peace, and even with a credible peace process that raises hope again, Iranian influence would be marginal at best, "resistance" organizations would lose appeal, and there would be few takers for ideological or material support from Iran.

The international community will also have to deal with the challenge of regional security in the Persian Gulf that cannot be restricted to, and is only partly related to, the problem of Iran's nuclear ambitions. The region is much too vital to the world economy and too volatile to simply wait and see whether regional actors at some point can come up with sustainable security arrangements among themselves. While it is noteworthy that even members of the Iranian policy community occasionally express fears that accidents between Iran and the United States, particularly between Iranian and U.S. naval vessels, could get out of hand, the challenge is not only one of bilateral U.S.-Iranian relations or communication.

As a midterm goal, regional states and international actors with strong interest and exposure in the region should therefore work toward establishing an inclusive, multilateral security arrangement for the Persian Gulf region. The international community should actively support any regional initiative that aims in this direction. That goes for the GCC initiative to establish a weapons-of-mass-destruction-free zone in the Persian Gulf. It should be explored among security experts and diplomats from regional states and other interested parties, even though it will probably not be achieved at an early stage.

Incrementalism may be the right approach to get things started. A regional security regime may eventually take the form of a stability and cooperation pact for the Persian Gulf, a loose structure with a secretariat and three or four regional panels for security, political cooperation, economic cooperation, and the environment. But it is unlikely to start as such: questions of membership and scope of such a regime will be controversial and will have to be sorted out in a diplomatic process. It may be advisable to use the Iraq Neighbors conferences to launch such a process. The states that have so far participated in these conferences should set up a working group as the diplomatic forum for official, midlevel explorations of these matters.

Practical cooperation could begin with confidence-building measures (CBMs) on issues of common concern such as the environment and fishery resources, the need to quickly react to oil spills, maritime security, and emergency rules for incidents at sea. CBMs could then extend to the exchange of information, coordination, and joint action in the fields of combating the illegal drug trade, arms trafficking, irregular migration, and human trafficking and also deal with border security issues.

The Persian Gulf states in particular need to find an agreement about the future role of international actors in regional security arrangements. While any regional regime will certainly have to involve Iran, Iraq, the GCC states, and Yemen as well as the United States, other international actors also have legitimate interests and some form of presence in the region. To bring in actors such as the EU, Russia, China, and India as well as the UN or the Arab League may not only be wise for what they can contribute materially and in terms of their experience, it will also give more legitimacy to the U.S. presence in such an arrangement.

What Iran Should Consider

Much of what has been said above with respect to the United States, Europe, or the international community at large finds the consent of interlocutors in the Iranian policy community. Listening to such partners, one sometimes gets the impression that, from their perspective, a resolution of the Iranian nuclear conflict—"nuclear issue," they would prefer to say—is entirely the responsibility of the United States, Europe, and probably some other major powers, and that basically the same applies to other conflicts and problems in which Iran has a stake. Iranian policymakers should avoid such a passive approach. Iran is the essential regional player in the Persian Gulf. It can trigger and heat up conflicts as well as contribute to their solution. Probably not everybody in the Iranian establishment has understood that being the regional lead power also brings responsibility and that only responsible behavior creates the kind of legitimacy and acceptance that Iran seeks among its neighbors. Iranian policymakers should therefore try to develop and present their own ideas for a negotiated resolution of the nuclear conflict and other security issues in the Middle East and think about how Iran could itself contribute to rebuilding trust.

Iranian leaders would be well advised to avoid hostile rhetoric. It is necessary for Tehran to realize how much the incendiary statements about Israel exacerbate the lack of trust among Iran's would-be partners and that such statements make it enormously difficult for those in Europe or the United States who are interested in building favorable relations or even a strong partnership with Iran. Iran is indicating that it wants to have a high-level dialogue with the United States in the not too distant future. It should realize that U.S. presidents have a domestic audience and that repeated violent statements about sensitive issues can easily set back even serious official attempts to get such a dialogue going.

Iran could also build up trust if it were to become more transparent, not least so about its own strategies and strategic ambitions. Why not publish such an essential document as Ayatollah Khamene'i's fatwa on nuclear weapons that is constantly referred to but unavailable? On quite another level, it might be a good thing for Iran to publish and reaffirm its twenty-year development plan in order to make clear what the country's strategic developmental goals are.

For a leading regional power like Iran, it would be even more helpful if it were to lay out its own strategic vision for the region. It should accept the concerns of its neighbors, seek to develop its own ideas for regional confidence and security building, and participate in efforts to create regional security arrangements. It should also positively respond to offers from Washington to establish some confidence-building measures between the two countries' military forces, particularly their navies.

With regard to the nuclear issue, Iran should try to switch from the language of principles and "inalienable rights" to one of pragmatic solutions. This would also help to depoliticize the issue. The right to independent nuclear research and development under the NPT is not disputed. But rather than insisting as a matter of principle on operating the fuel cycle independently and solely under national sovereignty, Iran could try to engage the Saudi government about their idea of a regional joint venture or explore different options of multilateral consortia with other countries. Iran's Parliament could make a strong contribution to confidence building and to the resolution of the nuclear conflict by ratifying the Additional Protocol.

Iran should spell out its ideas of a comprehensive partnership with Europe or of other regional and international partnerships. Would it be prepared to find a compromise that responds to European and other international concerns about its nuclear program and thereby gain the opportunity of wide-ranging economic, energy, technology, and science cooperation? Nuclear energy is only one technology, and it is a twentieth-century rather than a twenty-first-century one too. Eventually, such partnerships could help Iran to also become an economically leading power in the region and keep the best of its young generation in the country rather than having them queue for visas at foreign embassies in Tehran or, more often, the U.S. consulates in Istanbul or Dubai. All this depends on whether Iran defines its strength in terms of scientific research and economic and technological development or, instead, in military (or militarily usable) capacities.

Most important, Iran will have to decide what kind of actor on the regional and international scene it wants to be. Many options for cooperation and the willingness of major Western states to eventually accept Iran with a nuclear status like Japan's depend on whether Iran refers to itself as a status quo power, which its officials occasionally do, and also acts as such, or whether it acts instead as a disintegrative force.

If Iran wants to be seen as a status quo power, this demands, centrally, the preparedness to accept local and international efforts at establishing peace between Israel and its neighbors. Iran will not be required to recognize Israel: whether a state recognizes another is entirely up to its decision-making bodies. For a grand bargain with the United States, Iran would have to commit itself to cease its support for militant organizations like Hamas or Palestinian Islamic Jihad that undermine efforts at reaching a two-state solution for Israel and Palestine.

Even without such a bargain, however, Iran will have to do certain things if it wants to be seen as a constructive regional player. It will have to accept all other states in the region as legitimate players with their own legitimate interests, as much as it wants to be recognized as such itself. It would also have to accept, at the very least, the wish of the huge majority of the Palestinians to reach a peaceful settlement with Israel. Iranian officials have sometimes tried to temper more violent statements by President Ahmadinejad about the illegitimacy of Israel as nothing more than a call for "regime change" in the lands of Israel and Palestine. Even that would not exactly be a status quo policy. Iran is certainly entitled to seek assurances against externally forced regime change. It cannot have it both ways, though, seeking guarantees against regime change at home and promoting it in its neighborhood.

Final Caveats

As useful as it is to develop positive scenarios, we have to consider that they may not materialize. A regional-war scenario should not and cannot be totally discounted, but we are not going to explore it here. It is more likely, and quite possible, that no agreement about the nuclear issue will be found and that Iran and the international community will find themselves in a situation of prolonged stalemate without any diplomatic progress, a state of mutual blockade and noncooperation, probably punctuated by occasional unsuccessful attempts to resume negotiations as well as by repeated threats and mutual recriminations about the situation in Iraq or other parts of the region. Iran could become a sort of Cuba in the Middle East, a "Cuba," however, with a nuclear fuel cycle, perhaps with a latent military nuclear capability, midrange ballistic missiles, and quite some influence in Iraq and in other regional states. This would not be good for Iran nor for the world. There would be less political contact, less economic and societal interaction. The IAEA would have less control over the Iranian nuclear program than it would with an agreement that allowed limited Iranian fuel cycle activities with maximum safeguards. Opportunity costs for the international community and for Iran would be high. A more active integration of Iran into the world economy would remain far away. Whether Iran would openly acquire nuclear arms (which, as noted, is rather unlikely), rely on a latent military nuclear capability, or, instead, follow the Israeli example of nuclear ambiguity, the United States would certainly think about and employ all the instruments of cold war containment and deterrence, including military alliances or nuclear guarantees for its friends and perhaps even for neutral states in the region. At some point, most likely at the urging of its regional allies, another cold war toolbox would probably be opened, namely that of détente. Regional actors, with or without the support of Europe, Russia, and the United States, will start to consider confidence-building measures, regional security regimes, and arms control. There is nothing wrong with that. It would only be wiser to start such processes today.